LIBRARY AND INFORMATION SCIENCE

SECOND EDITION

Ferguson's
An Infobase Learning Company

Careers in Focus: Library and Information Science

Copyright © 2011 by Infobase Learning

Ferguson's
An imprint of Infobase Learning
132 West 31st Street
New York NY 10001

Library of Congress Cataloging-in-Publication Data

Careers in focus. Library & information science. — Second edition.
    pages cm
    At head of cover title: Ferguson's.
    Includes bibliographical references and index.
    ISBN-13: 978-0-8160-8032-8 (acid-free paper)
    ISBN-10: 0-8160-8032-1 (acid-free paper)   1. Library science—Vocational guidance—Juvenile literature.   2. Information science—Vocational guidance—Juvenile literature.   I. Ferguson Publishing.   II. Title: Library & information science.   III. Title: Library and information science.   IV. Title: Ferguson's careers in focus. Library & information science.
    Z682.35.V62C365 2011
    020'.23—dc22

                                                                    2010047035

Ferguson's books are available at special discounts when purchased in bulk quantities for businesses, associations, institutions, or sales promotions. Please call our Special Sales Department in New York at (212) 967-8800 or (800) 322-8755.

You can find Ferguson's on the World Wide Web at
http://www.infobaselearning.com

Text design by David Strelecky
Composition by Newgen North America
Cover printed by Yurchak Printing, Landisville, Penn.
Book printed and bound by Yurchak Printing, Landisville, Penn.
Date printed: April 2011
Printed in the United States of America

10 9 8 7 6 5 4 3 2 1

Table of Contents

Introduction

Information occupies an invaluable place in our lives. Information is the tool by which we learn, make decisions, and answer questions or concerns that we face every day at work, at school, and in our personal lives. A junior high school student may seek information on the history of ancient Greece to use in a school report. A college senior may look for technical information to help prepare for a job interview. A retired couple may gather information about the customs of a foreign country to help plan for a vacation trip. Parents may rely on information about low-cholesterol recipes to help create a healthier lifestyle for their family. A law librarian may compile information on previous legal cases in preparation for a court case. These are just a few examples of the different roles that information plays in the things we do and in the way we live.

The world of information is constantly changing and expanding. Each year more books—both print and electronic—are published, more articles appear in magazines or newspapers, new CD-ROMs and DVDs are produced, and more resources become available to us through computers by way of database vendors, online services, and access to the Internet. The growth and expansion of technology constantly create new ways for information to be preserved and new avenues for people to access information, whether through their own home computers, laptops, or tablet computers; on e-readers; on smartphones; in libraries; or in businesses or research institutes. But all this stored knowledge can be unwieldy and overwhelming. We need trained information professionals to help us organize and store the information in the first place, and then to provide guidance when we have to retrieve and synthesize the information.

Careers in Focus: Library and Information Science describes a variety of careers in the world of information and library science—in academic, corporate, medical, law, music, public, and other types of libraries; archives; colleges and universities; home offices; business offices; and countless other settings. These careers are as diverse in nature as they are in their earnings and educational requirements.

Salaries range from $16,000 for beginning research assistants to more than $119,000 for experienced library directors or $200,000 for self-employed information brokers with many years of experience.

Some careers, such as library assistants and technicians, require only a small amount of postsecondary training or an associate's degree but are excellent starting points for a career in the field.

Others—such as book conservators, database specialists, and research assistants—require a bachelor's degree. All librarian jobs, though, require a minimum of a master's degree in library science or library and information science. Doctoral degrees are often required for top library management positions and college professors.

The information services field is growing in more nontraditional settings. Cutbacks in library budgets will decrease opportunities for information services professionals, but the growth of our information-based society will counteract the decline. Easy access to recorded knowledge has become an essential part of life for information professionals in traditional libraries as well as for individuals, employees of research centers, professional firms, and businesses, and information brokers and research consultants.

Employment for librarians and library technicians and assistants is expected to increase about as fast as the average for all careers through 2018, according to the U.S. Department of Labor (DOL). Many libraries now assign technicians and assistants to perform tasks once handled exclusively by more highly paid professional librarians. Although this is partly a cost-cutting move, the reassignment of responsibilities allows librarians to dedicate more time to other responsibilities. However, computerized ordering, cataloging, and information retrieval programs require specialized training. Professional information scientists will continue to be necessary to direct, review, and coordinate such systems and to train and supervise operations.

Job prospects are expected to be best in privately financed special libraries. In addition, librarians with special qualifications, such as languages, computer services, or children's services, can anticipate better opportunities. Jobs requiring knowledge of science, mathematics, and business are considered difficult to fill because of fewer graduates with these backgrounds. Overall, the best opportunities for information services careers will be outside of the library, with private corporations, consulting businesses, and information brokers. Rather than being called librarians, these information professionals might be called *database specialists and trainers, systems analysts, Web developers, information architects,* or *local area network coordinators.*

In the future, libraries will increasingly become a part of a national network linking public, academic, and special libraries into one information source. Each library will retain its own identity and serve its own clientele, but information in any one location can be made available to patrons in any part of the country. Many systems, such as a central library catalog, perhaps supplemented by regional catalogs, will be made available by way of high-speed technology.

The information services industry is reflecting this trend toward linking information, and it is forging ahead to increase the opportunities created by the Internet. Expanding technologies of our society have made information part of a global network. As information continues to expand and to reach out to all corners of the earth, information services professionals will be needed to help these technologies make the world a much smaller and more easily accessible place.

Each article in this book discusses a particular library or information science occupation in detail. The articles in *Careers in Focus: Library and Information Science* appear in Ferguson's *Encyclopedia of Careers and Vocational Guidance*, but have been updated and revised with the latest information from the DOL, professional organizations, and other sources. The following paragraphs detail the career article sections and other features that appear in this book.

The **Quick Facts** section provides a brief summary of the career, including recommended school subjects, personal skills, work environment, minimum educational requirements, salary ranges, certification or licensing requirements, and employment outlook. This section also provides acronyms and identification numbers for the following government classification indexes: the Dictionary of Occupational Titles (DOT), the Guide for Occupational Exploration (GOE), the National Occupational Classification (NOC) Index, and the Occupational Information Network (O*NET)-Standard Occupational Classification System (SOC) index. The DOT, GOE, and O*NET-SOC indexes have been created by the U.S. government; the NOC index is Canada's career classification system. Readers can use the identification numbers listed in the Quick Facts section to access further information about a career. Print editions of the DOT (*Dictionary of Occupational Titles*. Indianapolis, Ind.: JIST Works, 1991) and GOE (*Guide for Occupational Exploration*. Indianapolis, Ind.: JIST Works, 2001) are available at libraries. Electronic versions of the DOT (http://www.oalj.dol.gov/libdot.htm), NOC (http://www5.hrsdc.gc.ca/NOC), and O*NET-SOC (http://online.onetcenter.org) are available on the Internet. When no DOT, GOE, NOC, or O*NET-SOC numbers are listed, this means that the U.S. Department of Labor or Human Resources and Skills Development Canada have not created a numerical designation for this career. In this instance, you will see the acronym "N/A," or not available.

The **Overview** section is a brief introductory description of the duties and responsibilities involved in this career. Oftentimes, a career may have a variety of job titles. When this is the case, alternative career titles are presented. Employment statistics are also provided, when available. The **History** section describes the history of the particular job as it relates to the overall development of its industry or field. **The Job** describes the primary and secondary duties of the job. **Requirements** discusses high school and postsecondary education and training requirements, any certification or licensing that is necessary, and other personal requirements for success in the job. **Exploring** offers suggestions on how to gain experience in or knowledge of the particular job before making a firm educational and financial commitment. The focus is on what can be done while still in high school (or in the early years of college) to gain a better understanding of the job. The **Employers** section gives an overview of typical places of employment for the job. **Starting Out** discusses the best ways to land that first job, be it through the college career services office, newspaper ads, Internet employment sites, or personal contact. The **Advancement** section describes what kind of career path to expect from the job and how to get there. **Earnings** lists salary ranges and describes the typical fringe benefits. The **Work Environment** section describes the typical surroundings and conditions of employment—whether indoors or outdoors, noisy or quiet, social or independent. Also discussed are typical hours worked, any seasonal fluctuations, and the stresses and strains of the job. The **Outlook** section summarizes the job in terms of the general economy and industry projections. For the most part, Outlook information is obtained from the U.S. Bureau of Labor Statistics and is supplemented by information gathered from professional associations. Job growth terms follow those used in the *Occupational Outlook Handbook*. Growth described as "much faster than the average" means an increase of 20 percent or more. Growth described as "faster than the average" means an increase of 14 to 19 percent. Growth described as "about as fast as the average" means an increase of 7 to 13 percent. Growth described as "more slowly than the average" means an increase of 3 to 6 percent. "Little or no change" means a decrease of 2 percent to an increase of 2 percent. "Decline" means a decrease of 3 percent or more. Each article ends with **For More Information,** which lists organizations that provide information on training, education, internships, scholarships, and job placement.

Careers in Focus: Library and Information Science also includes photos, informative sidebars, and interviews with professionals in the field.

Acquisition Librarians

OVERVIEW

Acquisition librarians build and maintain library collections, which include print references such as books and periodicals, and digital references such as CD-ROMs, PDFs, and DVDs, as well as music, art, and other resources available to library patrons. Acquisition librarians are also called *collection development librarians* and *collection development specialists*. Acquisition librarians are employed by all types of libraries, though the majority work in academic libraries.

HISTORY

Acquisitions and collection development has existed ever since the first library was created thousands of years ago. Early librarians acquired books, manuscripts, maps, and other materials to augment their existing collections. Today, acquisition librarians acquire not only books but periodicals, CD-ROMs, music, videos, films, electronic downloads, art, photographs, and other resources.

The Association for Library Collections and Technical Services (ALCTS), a division of the American Library Association (ALA), was formed in 1957 to serve the professional needs of acquisition librarians and related professionals.

QUICK FACTS

School Subjects
Business
Computer science

Personal Skills
Helping/teaching
Leadership/management

Work Environment
Primarily indoors
Primarily one location

Minimum Education Level
Master's degree

Salary Range
$30,000 to $53,710 to $120,000+

Certification or Licensing
None available

Outlook
About as fast as the average

DOT
100

GOE
12.03.04

NOC
5111

O*NET-SOC
25-4021.00

THE JOB

Acquisition librarians are responsible for building and maintaining a library's collection of books and periodicals (including e-publications), CD-ROMs, music, videos, and other resources

Books to Read

Bell, Suzanne S. *Librarian's Guide to Online Searching.* 2d ed. Santa Barbara, Calif.: Libraries Unlimited, 2009.

De La Peña McCook, Kathleen. *Opportunities in Library and Information Science.* 3d ed. New York: McGraw-Hill, 2008.

Eckstrand, Tatyana. *The Librarian's Book of Quotes.* Chicago: American Library Association, 2009.

Johnson, Marilyn. *This Book Is Overdue!: How Librarians and Cybrarians Can Save Us All.* New York: Harper, 2010.

Murray, Richard, and Priscilla K. Shontz. *A Day in the Life: Career Options in Library and Information Science.* Santa Barbara, Calif.: Libraries Unlimited, 2007.

Sommer, Deb. *Vault Guide to Library Careers.* New York: Vault Inc., 2009.

available for use. They must be able to balance the wants and needs of library patrons with the limitations of their budget. They work with library directors to assess the needs of the library and determine how to best allocate financial resources. Acquisition librarians rely on reviews in trade publications, information gathered at trade shows, suggestions from patrons, and the Internet to help them make purchasing decisions.

Changing technology has created new challenges for acquisition librarians; not only has information become more readily accessible with the advent and popularity of the Internet, it also comes in new formats. Acquisition librarians must determine what format is best for each resource. For example, they may choose to purchase a magazine subscription in online format to save storage space or to allow more people to access the resource. Or they may prefer hard copies of a particularly popular reference material if there is a shortage of computer terminals in the library.

In order to know what items are needed within the library, acquisition librarians must first be familiar with the resources that are currently held within the library. They work with cataloging and circulation librarians to find out what items are most popular and which ones might need to be replaced due to wear and tear or oversights in prior purchasing. They may even help these librarians catalog and maintain existing resources, conduct repair work on used items, and assess which books, magazines, and other items need to be replaced.

When budget limitations restrict purchasing, some acquisition librarians seek out other sources of funding. They may write grants for public or private funding or lead donation drives to add to their collection.

REQUIREMENTS
High School
To prepare for this career, take college preparatory classes in business, science, English, mathematics, and foreign language. And take as many computer classes as you can. Because technology has greatly changed the way we receive and store information, those familiar with computers and related technology will have the greatest professional success.

Postsecondary Training
Most acquisition librarian positions require a master's degree in library science (M.L.S.), a master's degree in library information service, or a master of science in information science. Some acquisition librarians may even hold a Ph.D. in information or library science. A graduate degree from a program accredited by the ALA is highly regarded by employers. Some schools, such as the University at Albany-State University of New York (http://www.albany.edu/informationstudies/index.php), offer a 10-semester program that combines a bachelor's degree in arts or science with a master of library science or master of information science. Participants also complete an internship at colleges and universities, other schools, companies such as IBM, hospitals, newspapers, banks, and law libraries. Visit the ALA Web site, http://ala.org, for a list of accredited schools nationwide, as well as distance learning opportunities, scholarships, and financial aid.

Certification or Licensing
To date, there are no certification requirements for this library specialty. However, many librarians rely on annual conferences and continuing education classes to advance their knowledge. The ALCTS, for example, offers an online course on acquisition fundamentals. Topics include methods and basic functions of acquisitions, ethics, and creating and following a budget.

Other Requirements
Acquisition librarians should first and foremost have a love of information, as they are constantly in search of ways to improve their

library's collection and provide its patrons with useful resources. They should also have strong computer skills, be good at solving problems, and have business acumen to negotiate contracts and licenses for certain materials, such as e-subscriptions. Acquisition librarians need strong communication skills since they work closely with library patrons, vendors, the library director, and other library professionals.

EXPLORING

There are many ways to learn more about the career of acquisition librarian. You can read books and magazines about librarianship and visit the Web sites of library associations. (LibraryCareers.org, http://www.ala.org/ala/educationcareers/careers/librarycareerssite/home.cfm, which is sponsored by the ALA, is one good starting point.) You might also visit the Web sites of library acquisitions departments to learn about issues that affect acquisition librarians. Ask your school librarian about the acquisition or collection development aspects of his or her job. A librarian, teacher, or school counselor may be able to arrange an information interview with an acquisition librarian. Contact professional associations to see if they offer memberships for students or the general public. For example, the ALA offers a membership options for nonlibrarians who are "interested in participating in the work of the association."

EMPLOYERS

The Association for Library Collections and Technical Services, the major professional association for acquisition librarians, has nearly 5,000 members. According to the association, 75 percent of its members work in academic libraries and 11 percent in public libraries. The remaining 14 percent work in special libraries and other settings.

STARTING OUT

To break into this career, turn to library association Web sites or publications for job listings and recruiters. The ALA job Web site, http://joblist.ala.org, for example, offers links to employment opportunities throughout the country, as posted by different library organizations. The ALA also offers a career guidance Web site, http://www.getajob.ala.org, that provides tips on landing a job. It would also be prudent to check with your school's career services office.

Many employers work closely with academic institutions, especially if their programs are well regarded. Let your counselor know your area of specialty early on so he or she can help you find an internship or full-time job best suited to your needs.

ADVANCEMENT

Acquisition librarians with experience and advanced degrees may become managers of acquisitions departments or library directors. Others advance laterally by seeking employment at libraries with larger collections or facilities. Some acquisition librarians become library science educators at the postsecondary level.

EARNINGS

According to StateUniversity.com, annual salaries for acquisition librarians varied from $30,000 for entry-level positions to $120,000 or more for experienced acquisition librarians working for the federal government or universities. The U.S. Department of Labor (DOL) reports that the median annual salary for all librarians in 2009 was $53,710. Most acquisition librarians receive paid vacation time, holiday pay, compensated sick leave, various insurance plans, and retirement savings programs.

WORK ENVIRONMENT

Acquisition librarians work in an intellectually engaging and fast-paced environment. The work can be challenging at times, as they must satisfy a variety of requests from patrons—from a student seeking an obscure book on medieval cooking to educators requesting a new series of historical biographies. Acquisition librarians must be able to maintain their concentration and focus as they move from a critical budget meeting with the library director, to interacting with library patrons, to making the rounds at an important book fair, to poring over a new stack of publisher's reviews.

OUTLOOK

The DOL predicts that employment for all librarians will grow about as fast as the average for all careers through 2018. Opportunities for acquisition librarians should also be good. Today, libraries offer a wide variety of materials—including books, periodicals, electronic publications and music, CD-ROMs, music, and videos—to patrons, and acquisition librarians will be needed to assess and acquire these materials. Opportunities will be best at libraries with large collections and a variety of media.

FOR MORE INFORMATION

For information on careers in law librarianship, contact
American Association of Law Libraries
105 West Adams Street, Suite 3300
Chicago, IL 60603-6225
Tel: 312-939-4764
http://www.aallnet.org

For a list of accredited schools and information on careers, scholarships and grants, and membership, contact
American Library Association
50 East Huron Street
Chicago, IL 60611-2729
Tel: 800-545-2433
http://www.ala.org

To learn more about information science careers, contact
American Society for Information Science and Technology
1320 Fenwick Lane, Suite 510
Silver Spring, MD 20910-3560
Tel: 301-495-0900
E-mail: asis@asis.org
http://www.asis.org

For more information on careers in this field, contact
Association for Library Collections and Technical Services
50 East Huron Street
Chicago, IL 60611-2795
Tel: 800-545-2433, ext. 5037
E-mail: alcts@ala.org
http://www.ala.org/ala/mgrps/divs/alcts

For information on careers in medical librarianship, contact
Medical Library Association
65 East Wacker Place, Suite 1900
Chicago, IL 60601-7246
Tel: 312-419-9094
E-mail: info@mlahq.org
http://www.mlanet.org

For information on careers in music librarianship, contact
Music Library Association
8551 Research Way, Suite 180
Middleton, WI 53562-3567
Tel: 608-836-5825
E-mail: mla@areditions.com
http://www.musiclibraryassoc.org

For information on working in a specialized library, contact
Special Libraries Association
331 South Patrick Street
Alexandria, VA 22314-3501
Tel: 703-647-4900
http://www.sla.org

To receive information on librarianship in Canada, contact
Canadian Library Association
1150 Morrison Drive, Suite 400
Ottawa, ON K2H 8S9 Canada
Tel: 613-232-9625
E-mail: info@cla.ca
http://www.cla.ca

Archivists

QUICK FACTS

School Subjects
English
Foreign language
History

Personal Skills
Communication/ideas
Leadership/management

Work Environment
Primarily indoors
Primarily one location

Minimum Education Level
Master's degree

Salary Range
$27,050 to $46,470 to
$78,680+

Certification or Licensing
Voluntary

Outlook
About as fast as the average

DOT
101

GOE
12.03.04

NOC
5113

O*NET-SOC
25-4011.00

OVERVIEW

Archivists contribute to the study of the arts and sciences by analyzing, acquiring, and preserving historical documents, artwork, organizational and personal records, and information systems that are significant enough to be preserved for future generations. Archivists keep track of artifacts such as letters, contracts, films, photographs, video and sound recordings, electronic data files, blueprints, and other items of potential historical significance. Approximately 6,300 archivists are employed in the United States.

HISTORY

For centuries, archives have served as repositories for the official records of governments, educational institutions, businesses, religious organizations, families, and countless other groups. From the first time information was recorded, there has been a need to preserve those accounts. The evolution of archiving information in a manner similar to what we know today can be traced back to the Middle Ages.

As the feudal system in Europe gave way to nations and a more systematic order of law, precise record keeping became increasingly important to keep track of land ownership and official policy. These records helped governments serve the needs of their citizens and protected the rights of the common people in civil matters.

In America, early settlers maintained records using skills they brought from their European homelands. Families kept records of the journey to their new country and saved correspondence with family members still in Europe. Religious institutions kept records

Employment/Earnings for Archivists by Industry, 2009

Employer	Employment	Mean Earnings
Colleges and universities	1,020	$46,460
Museums and historical sites	940	$42,960
State government	700	$45,430
Federal government	410	$78,760
Other information services	400	$56,460

Source: U.S. Department of Labor

of the births, deaths, and marriages of their members. Settlers kept track of their business transactions, such as land purchases, crop trades, and building constructions.

In the early 18th century, similar to what occurred in Europe in the Middle Ages, civic records in America became more prevalent as towns became incorporated. Leaders needed to maintain accurate records of property ownership and laws made by and for citizens.

Although archives have been incorporated in one form or another for centuries, archivists have established themselves as professionals only in the last 125 years or so. In the past, museums and societies accumulated records and objects rapidly and sometimes indiscriminately, accepting items regardless of their actual merit. Each archive had its own system of documenting, organizing, and storing materials. In 1884, the American Historical Association was formed to develop archival standards and help boost interaction among archivists.

Each year, as new scientific discoveries are made and new works are published, the need for sifting through and classifying items increases. More advanced computer systems will help archivists catalog archival materials as well as make archives more readily available to users. Advances in conservation techniques will help extend the life of fragile items, allowing them to be available to future generations.

THE JOB

Archivists analyze documents and materials such as government records, minutes of corporate board meetings, letters from famous people, charters of nonprofit foundations, historical photographs, maps, coins, works of art, and nearly anything else that may have historical significance. To determine which documents should be saved, they consider such factors as when the resource was written, who wrote it, and for whom it was written. In deciding on other items to archive, the archivist needs to consider the provenance, or history of creation and ownership, of the materials. They also take into account the physical capacity of their employer's archives. For instance, a repository with very little space for new materials may need to decline the gift of a large or bulky item, despite its potential value.

Archives are kept by various organizations, including government agencies, corporations, universities, and museums, and the value of documents is generally dictated by whichever group owns them. For example, the U.S. Army may not be interested in General Motors' corporate charter, and General Motors may not be interested in a Civil War battle plan. Archivists understand and serve the needs of their employers and collect items that are most relevant to their organizations.

Archivists may also be in charge of collecting items of historical significance to the institution for which they work. An archivist at a university, for instance, may collect new copies of the student newspaper to keep historical documentation of student activities and issues up-to-date. An archivist at a public library may prepare, present, and store annual reports of the branch libraries in order to keep an accurate record of library statistics.

After selecting appropriate materials, archivists help make them accessible to others by preparing reference aids such as indexes, guides, bibliographies, descriptions, and microfilmed copies of documents. These research aids may be printed and kept in the organization's stack area, put online so off-site researchers have access to the information, or put on CD-ROM for distribution to other individuals or organizations. Archivists also file and cross-index archived items for easy retrieval when a user wishes to consult a collection.

Archivists may preserve and repair historical documents or send damaged items to a professional conservator. They may also appraise the items based on their knowledge of political, economic, military, and social history, as well as by the materials' physical condition, research potential, and rarity.

Archivists play an integral role in the exhibition programs of their organizations. A university library, for instance, may present an exhibit that honors former Nobel Prize-winning faculty members. Most accomplished faculty members leave their papers—notes, research, experiments, and articles—to their institutions. An

An archivist at the Mark Twain Archive at Elmira College holds a first edition of *The Adventures of Huckleberry Finn*, by Mark Twain. *(David Duprey, AP Photo)*

exhibition might display first drafts of articles, early versions of experiments, or letters between two distinguished scientists debating some aspect of a project's design. Exhibits allow members of the university and the community to learn about the history of an organization and how research has advanced the field. The archivist helps to sort through archival materials and decide what items would make for an interesting exhibition at the institution.

Many archivists conduct research using the archival materials at their disposal, and they may publish articles detailing their findings. They may advise government agencies, scholars, journalists, and others conducting research by supplying available materials and information. Archivists also act as reference contacts and teachers. An employee doing research at the company archives may have little knowledge of how and where to begin. The archivist may suggest that the worker consult specific reference guides or browse through an online catalog. After the employee decides which materials will be of most use, the archivist may retrieve the archives from storage, circulate the collection to the user, and perhaps even instruct the user as to the proper handling of fragile or oversize materials.

Archivists may have assistants who help them sort and index archival collections. At a university library, undergraduate or graduate students usually act as archival assistants. Small community historical societies may rely on trained volunteers to assist the archivist.

Depending on the size of their employing organization, archivists may perform many or few administrative duties. Such duties may include preparing budgets, representing their institutions at scientific or association conferences, soliciting support for institutions, and interviewing and hiring personnel. Some help formulate and interpret institutional policy. In addition, archivists may plan or participate in special research projects and write articles for scientific journals.

REQUIREMENTS

High School

If you are interested in doing archival work, high school is not too early to begin your training. Since it is usually necessary to earn a master's degree to become an archivist, you should select a college preparatory curriculum in high school and plan on going to college. While in high school, you should pay special attention to learning library and research skills. Classes in English, history, science, and mathematics will provide you with basic skills and knowledge for university study. Journalism courses will help you hone your research skills, and political science courses will help you identify events of societal importance. Since many archives are becoming electronic, computer science and Web technology classes will be especially useful. You should also plan on learning at least one foreign language. If you are interested in doing archival work at a religious organization, Latin or Hebrew may be good language options. If you would like to work in a specialized archive, such as an art gallery or medical school archive, you should also focus on classes that will prepare you for that specialty.

Postsecondary Training

To prepare for archival work in college, you should get a bachelor's degree in the liberal arts. You will probably want to study history, library science, or a related field, since there are currently no undergraduate programs that deal solely with the archival sciences. You should take any specific courses in archival methods that are available to you as an undergraduate.

Since many employers prefer to hire archivists with a graduate degree, consider any course load that may help you gain entrance into a program to earn a master's degree in library and information science or history. A few colleges offer master's degrees in archival science. Graduate school will give you the opportunity to learn more specific details about archival work. These courses will teach you how to do many aspects of archival work, from selecting items and organizing collections to preparing documentation and conserving materials. While in graduate school, you may be able to secure a part-time job or assistantship at your school's archives. Many university archives rely on their own students to provide valuable help maintaining collections, and students who work there gain firsthand knowledge and experience in the archival field.

The Society of American Archivists offers a list of educational programs at its Web site, http://www.archivists.org/prof-education/edd-index.asp.

Many positions require a second master's degree in a specific field or a doctorate degree. An archivist at a historical society may need a master's degree in history and another master's in library and information science. Candidates with bachelor's degrees may serve as assistants while they complete their formal training.

Certification or Licensing
Although not currently required by most employers, voluntary certification for archivists is available from the Academy of Certified Archivists. Certification is earned by gaining practical experience in archival work, taking requisite courses, and passing an examination on the history, theory, and practice of archival science. Archivists need to renew their certification status every five years, usually by examination. Certification can be especially useful to archivists wishing to work in the corporate world.

Other Requirements
Archivists need to have excellent research and organizational skills. They should be comfortable working with rare and fragile materials. They need to maintain archives with absolute discretion, especially in the case of closed archives or archives available only for specific users. Archivists also need to be able to communicate effectively with all types of people who may use the archives, since they will be explaining the research methods and the policies and procedures of their organization. Finally, archivists may be required to move heavy boxes and other awkward materials. An archivist should be comfortable lifting or carrying large objects, although requirements may be different for various organizations and arrangements can often be made for professionals with different abilities.

EXPLORING

If you are interested in archival work, a good way to learn about the field is by using archives for your own research. If you have a report due on Abraham Lincoln, for instance, you could visit an archive near your home that houses some of Lincoln's personal papers and letters. A visit to the archives of a candy manufacturer could help you with an assignment on the history of a specific type of production method. Since institutions may limit access to their collections, be sure to contact the organization about your project before you make the trip.

Getting to know an archivist can give you a good perspective of the field and the specific duties of the professional archivist. You could also see if a professional archival or historical association offers special student memberships or mentoring opportunities.

You can also learn more about archival work by creating your own family archive consisting of letters, birth and marriage certificates, old photographs, special awards, and any other documents that would help someone understand your family's history.

Another way to gain practical experience is to obtain part-time or volunteer positions in archives, historical societies, or libraries. Many museums and cultural centers train volunteer guides (who are called *docents*) to give tours of their institutions. If you already volunteer for an organization in another capacity, ask to have a personal tour of the archives.

EMPLOYERS

Approximately 6,300 archivists are employed in the United States. Archivists can find employment in various fields. About 18 percent of the nation's archivists are employed in government positions, working for the Department of Defense, the National Archives and Records Administration, and other state and federal repositories. Approximately 16 percent of archivists work in academia, working in college and university libraries; and approximately 15 percent of archivists work in positions for museums, historical societies, and similar institutions. Others work for zoos or for private, not-for-profit archives that serve special interests, such as the Lesbian Herstory Archives in New York.

Archivists are also on staff at corporations, religious institutions, and professional associations. Many of these organizations need archivists to manage massive amounts of records that will be kept for posterity, or to comply with state or federal regulations. Some private collectors may also employ an archivist to process, organize, and catalog their personal holdings.

STARTING OUT

There is no best way to become an archivist. Since only a few colleges and universities offer degrees in archival science, many people working in the field today have had to pave their own way. For example, some archivists may begin by earning a master's degree in history and then a Ph.D. in history or a related field. They may go on to process collections in their university's archives. By enhancing their educational credentials with practical experience in the field, new archivists can gradually move on to positions with greater degrees of responsibility.

Another archivist may approach his or her career from a different direction. For example, an archivist could start out with a master's degree in French and then earn a master's of library science (M.L.S.) degree, with a concentration in archival management. With a language background and the M.L.S., he or she could begin working in archival positions in colleges and universities.

Candidates for positions as archivists should apply to institutions for entry-level positions only after completing their undergraduate degrees—usually in history. An archivist going into a particular area of archival work, however, may wish to earn a degree in that field. If you are interested in working in a museum's archives, for instance, you may wish to pursue a degree in art or art history.

Many potential archivists choose to work part time as research assistants, interns, or volunteers in order to gain archival experience. School career services offices are good starting points to look for research assistantships and internships. Professional librarian and archivist associations often have job listings for those new to the field.

ADVANCEMENT

Archivists usually work in small sections, units, or departments, so internal promotion opportunities are often limited. Promising archivists advance by gaining more responsibility for the administration of the collections. They may begin to spend more time supervising the work of others. Archivists can also advance by transferring to larger repositories and taking more administration-based positions.

Because the best jobs as archivists are contingent upon education, the surest method of advancement is through pursuing advanced or specialized degrees. Ambitious archivists should also attend conferences and workshops to stay current with developments in their fields. Archivists can enhance their status by conducting independent research and publishing their findings. In a public or private library, an archivist may move on to a position such as curator, chief librarian, or library director.

Archivists may also move outside of the standard archival field entirely. With their background and skills, archivists may become teachers, university professors, or instructors at a library school. They may also set up shop for themselves as archival consultants to corporations or private collectors.

EARNINGS

Salaries for archivists vary considerably by institution and may depend on education and experience. People employed by the federal government or by prestigious museums generally earn more than those working for small organizations. The U.S. Department of Labor (DOL) reports that the median annual salary for all archivists was $46,470 in 2009. The lowest paid 10 percent earned $27,050 or less, while the highest paid 10 percent earned $78,680 or more. In 2009, archivists employed by the federal government earned average annual salaries of $83,758.

Archivists who work for large corporations, institutions, or government agencies generally receive a full range of benefits, including health care coverage, vacation days, paid holidays, paid sick time, and retirement savings plans. Self-employed archival consultants usually have to provide their own benefits. All archivists have the added benefit of working with rare and unique materials. They have the opportunity to work with history and create documentation of the past.

WORK ENVIRONMENT

Because dirt, sunlight, and moisture can damage materials and documents, archivists generally work in clean, climate-controlled surroundings with artificial lighting rather than windows. Many archives are small offices, often employing the archivist alone, or with one or two part-time volunteers. Other archives are part of a larger department within an organization. The archives for DePaul University in Chicago, for instance, are part of the special collections and archives department and are managed by the curator. With this type of arrangement, the archivist generally has a number of graduate assistants to help with the processing of materials and departmental support staff to assist with clerical tasks.

Archivists often have little opportunity for physical activity, save for the bending, lifting, and reaching they may need to do in order to arrange collections and make room for new materials. Also, some archival collections include not only paper records but some oversized items as well. The archives of an elite fraternal organization, for example, may house a collection of hats or uniforms that members wore throughout the years, each of which must be processed, cataloged, preserved, and stored.

Most archivists work 40 hours a week, usually during regular, weekday working hours. Depending on the needs of their department and the community they serve, an archive may be open some weekend hours, thus requiring the archivist to be on hand for users. Also, archivists spend some of their time traveling to the homes of donors to view materials that may complement an archival collection.

OUTLOOK

Job opportunities for archivists are expected to increase about as fast as the average for all careers through 2018, according to the DOL. But since qualified job applicants outnumber the positions available, competition for jobs as archivists is keen. Candidates with specialized training, such as master's degrees in history and library science, will have better opportunities. A doctorate in history or a related field can also be a boon to job-seeking archivists. Graduates who have studied archival work or records management and who specialize in electronic records and records management will be in higher demand than those without that background. Also, by gaining related work or volunteer experience, many potential archivists will be in a better position to find full-time employment.

Jobs are expected to increase as more corporations and private organizations establish an archival history. Archivists will also be needed to fill positions left vacant by retirees and archivists who leave the occupation. On the other hand, budget cuts in educational institutions, museums, and cultural institutions often reduce demand for archivists. Overall, there will always be positions available for archivists, but the aspiring archivist may need to be creative, flexible, and determined in forging a career path.

FOR MORE INFORMATION

To find out about archival certification procedures, contact
Academy of Certified Archivists
1450 Western Avenue, Suite 101
Albany, NY 12203-3539
Tel: 518-694-8471
http://www.certifiedarchivists.org

For information about archival programs, activities, and publications in North America, contact
American Institute for Conservation of Historic and Artistic
    Works
1156 15th Street, NW, Suite 320
Washington DC 20005-1714
Tel: 202-452-9545
E-mail: info@conservation-us.org
http://www.conservation-us.org

If you are interested in working with the archives of film and television, contact
Association of Moving Image Archivists
1313 North Vine Street
Hollywood, CA 90028-8107
Tel: 323-463-1500
E-mail: amia@amianet.org
http://amianet.org

For information on archivists who are employed by government agencies, contact
National Association of Government Archives and Records
    Administrators
1450 Western Avenue, Suite 101
Albany, NY 12203-3539
Tel: 518-463-8644
E-mail: nagara@caphill.com
http://www.nagara.org

For a list of educational programs and to read So You Want to Be
an Archivist: An Overview of the Archival Profession, *visit the SAA
Web site.*
Society of American Archivists (SAA)
17 North State Street, Suite 1425
Chicago, IL 60602-3315
Tel: 866-722-7858
E-mail: servicecenter@archivists.org
http://www.archivists.org

*For information about archival programs and activities in Canada,
contact*
Association of Canadian Archivists
PO Box 2596, Station D

Ottawa, ON K1P 5W6 Canada
Tel: 613-234-6977
E-mail: aca@archivists.ca
http://archivists.ca

For information on archival work and publications in the United Kingdom, contact
Society of Archivists
Prioryfield House
20 Canon Street
Taunton, Somerset
TA1 1SW England
http://www.archives.org.uk

Book Conservators

QUICK FACTS

School Subjects
Art
History

Personal Skills
Artistic
Mechanical/manipulative

Work Environment
Primarily indoors
Primarily one location

Minimum Education Level
Bachelor's degree

Salary Range
$23,530 to $37,120 to
$67,090+

Certification or Licensing
Voluntary

Outlook
About as fast as the average

DOT
102

GOE
12.03.04

NOC
5112

O*NET-SOC
25-4013.00

OVERVIEW

Book conservators treat the bindings and pages of books and nonbook items to help preserve original materials for future use. Their work often includes removing a book block from its binding, sewing, measuring, gluing, rebinding, and using special chemical treatments to maintain the integrity of the item. Most conservators work in libraries, in museums, or for special conservation centers.

HISTORY

In order to understand the history of book conservation as a field, it is important to learn something about the evolution of books and bookbinding. Early books were not bound, but rather rolled, such as ancient Egyptian papyrus rolls and early Christian parchment rolls. Eventually the rolls were cut into a number of flat panels sewn together along one edge, thus allowing for a book that was more convenient, portable, and enduring. Early Latin codex manuscripts were made up of folded sheets gathered into signatures, or groups of folded pages, and sewn together. Wooden boards were then placed on either side of the sewn signatures. In time, the entire volume was covered with leather or other animal skins to hide the sewing cords and provide protection to the pages. The basic constructional elements of bookbinding have changed little in the past 1,800 years, but the materials and methods used have matured considerably.

Before the invention of the printing press, religious orders were often charged with copying texts by hand. These same monastic groups also assumed the roles of bookbinder and conservator. One

The Rise of E-Books

Electronic books (often known as e-books) are becoming increasingly popular among students, according to a survey by ebrary. Fifty-one percent of students reported that they "very often" or "often" used e-books instead of print editions. Only 32 percent of respondents said that they "sometimes" preferred e-books over print editions. Seventeen percent said they always used print copies.

Source: ebrary, 2008 Global Student E-book Survey

of the main goals in creating books is the conservation and dissemination of knowledge.

In order to pass that knowledge on to future generations, many early bookbinders began the legacy of conservation by using high-quality materials and excellent craftsmanship. A book that is well crafted in the first place will need less invasive conservation as the material ages. Historically, then, the people who created the books had the specialized knowledge to conserve them.

Conservators today are often from the same mold as early bookbinders. They have the specialized knowledge of how books have traditionally been crafted, and they use technologically advanced adhesives, papers, and binding techniques to ensure that materials created centuries ago will be around for years to come.

The establishment of book conservation as a career field apart from bookbinding probably began when the first courses in conservation and preservation were taught at a library school, or when a professional library association first addressed the topic. Thus, although early bookbinders dealt with issues of material longevity, conservation as a field has only been around for 100 years or so.

THE JOB

Book conservators work to slow down or stabilize the deterioration of books and other print-based materials. They repair books that have been damaged by misuse, accident, pests, or normal wear and tear; treat items that may have been produced or repaired with inferior materials or methods; and work to ensure that the books will be around for the future.

Before beginning any conservation efforts, book conservators must examine the item to be restored, determine the extent and cause of the deterioration, evaluate their own conservation skills, and decide on a proper course of action. In deciding how to treat an item, the book conservator must first consider the history of the item. When was it made? Book conservators must have a good knowledge of the history of bookmaking in order to serve the needs of the item. A book bound by hand in Italy in 1600 will have different needs than a volume bound by machine in 1980.

The book conservator also needs to consider what other repairs have been made to the book over the years. Sometimes a shoddy repair job in the past can create more work for today's conservator. For example, someone 30 years ago may have taped a torn page to keep it from ripping out entirely. Unfortunately, this hasty action, coupled with tape that will not stand the test of time, could lead to cracked, yellowing tape and stained book pages. When repairing a ripped sheet, book conservators use a pH-neutral (acid-free) adhesive, such as wheat paste, and Japanese paper or a special acid-free book tape. Since high levels of acidity in papers and materials increase the rate of deterioration, all materials that conservators use must be acid-free and of archival quality.

Book conservators also think about the current and future use of the book. For a common, high-use volume that will be checked out of the library frequently, they may repair the book with cheaper, lower quality materials that will survive being tossed into a backpack and repeated trips through the return chute. For a textbook that is reprinted each year, for example, a thick piece of tape may be an adequate conservation method. If such a book is falling out of its cover, the conservator may need to remove the book block entirely, repair or replace the end sheets and headbands, and reglue the book block back into the cover. If the cover of the book is broken, the conservator may need to fit the text block into a new cover. This involves measuring out the binder's board and book cloth, cutting the materials to size, gluing the cloth onto the board, sizing in the book block, and then finally gluing and setting the book. After the glue is dry, the conservator will inspect the item to ensure that all materials were fitted in properly, and that all problems were corrected.

Rare books that are handled less frequently or only by specially trained users can have less invasive repairs in order to maintain the integrity of the original item. For instance, a conservator may choose to make a box to house a book rather than repair a broken spine. If the conservation work would lessen the value of the book, sometimes it's better to simply stop the deterioration rather than repair the damage.

Book conservators clean books that were soaked by a flood. Some rare and valuable books were treated immediately after cleaning in order to prevent their decomposition. Specialists later examined and conserved them piece by piece. *(Stan Peska, CTK/AP Photo)*

The historical and monetary value of a book is a key factor in deciding upon treatment. As with any antique, often less restoration is more. On a recent antiques television program, an owner refinished an antique table and thereby reduced its resale value by thousands of dollars. The same can be said for books. Many old and rare books have great value because of the historical materials and methods in evidence.

Sometimes pests are encountered in conservation work. Beetle larvae and other insects may feast upon crumbs left in books, the pulp of the paper, or the adhesive, and make holes in the text. The conservator will assess the extent of the damage and prescribe a treatment. For critter damage to books, the most important thing is to ensure that any infestation is under control. The conservator needs to make sure that all bugs in a book are dead; if not, the items may need to be taken to a professional for fumigation. Once that is complete, the conservator can look at possible repair options. If the damage is under control, the conservator will probably opt for further damage prevention in lieu of repair.

Often conservators treat books for only part of their day. They might also spend much time working on ways to minimize the need for conservation and repair work in the first place. Book conservators who work as part of a large department have other duties, such as dealing with patrons, reference work, security, training assistants, fielding calls from the public, giving seminars, and teaching. Conservators may also serve on groups and committees devoted to preservation, conservation, and the administration of a conservation lab or department.

REQUIREMENTS

High School
You should plan on taking a college preparatory course load while in high school. Classes such as history, literature, art, foreign languages, chemistry, and mathematics will all help you build a strong background for book conservation. By studying history, you can learn the social and historical contexts of books and knowledge. Understanding the history of an item can give you a better perspective on approaching the material as a conservator. Strong knowledge of literature can help you appraise the potential value of a book. A comprehension of foreign languages allows you to deal with a wider variety of books from around the globe. Chemistry and math will begin to teach you about the composition and measurement of the materials you will be using. Art will teach you how to use your hands to create beautiful works that last.

Postsecondary Training

In the past, book conservators gained their training by participating in an apprenticeship or internship. Today, graduate programs in book conservation have become the primary method of training to enter this field, although some students still enter this field after earning a bachelor's degree and completing an apprenticeship or internship to round out their training. A bachelor's degree in art, art history, or one of the fine arts may help you gain entry into a book conservation apprenticeship or internship program. Your school may offer courses, or even an undergraduate degree, in the book or paper arts, which often include classes in preservation and conservation. You will also need to take courses that help you learn how to select items for conservation, how to purchase and best utilize your conservation materials, and how to prepare documentation on your conservation methods and treatments.

Upon earning a bachelor's degree, you should attend a graduate school that offers training in book conservation. These programs are commonly offered by the art conservation departments of academic institutions. Some students may wish to attend library school to earn a master's degree in library science with a concentration in book and document conservation. Again, advanced degrees may not be necessary for some positions, but they can always help you gain more prominent positions—particularly in administration—and perhaps command a higher salary. Additionally, any special skills you gain through advanced education will make you more attractive to potential employers and private clients.

Certification or Licensing

Some book conservators gain certification from their library school or from professional organizations such as the Academy of Certified Archivists. The certification process generally requires a mix of formal study of theory and practice, as well as a certain amount of actual experience in the field. Certification is not officially required by any federal, state, or local agencies, but some employers may request, or require, a certified book conservationist for particular positions or projects. Also, certifying organizations compile a list of all their certified conservators. If someone contacts an organization looking for a conservator, the agency will refer the client to member book conservators in the area.

Other Requirements

Book conservators need be able to think creatively. Conservation projects require the conservator to visualize the end product before beginning work. Conservators should enjoy problem solving and be able to decide the best way to conserve the materials. Having a hands-on nature is key as well, since book conservators spend a majority of their time inspecting materials and making repairs by hand.

Since book conservators routinely work with musty, moldy, and mildewed books, they should not be overly sensitive to odors. They also deal with sharp instruments, such as awls, knives, and paper cutters, so for safety reasons they should have a certain amount of facility with their hands. Book conservators also work with adhesives and chemicals, so they must take care not to spill materials.

Although much of their day is spent working with the materials, many conservators deal with the public as well. Book conservators, therefore, should be able to communicate well, and with a certain measure of tact, with many types of people. They should be able to explain conservation options to clients and to best determine what procedures will meet the needs of the material and the owner.

EXPLORING

If you are interested in becoming a book conservator, you should start out by learning all you can about how books are made. Study the history of books and of binding. Purchase an inexpensive, hardcover book at a used bookstore and take it apart to see how the book block is sewn together and how it is connected to the cover. Then try to put the book back together. There are many "how to" bookbinding guides to help you. Check out *Hand Bookbinding: A Manual of Instruction*, by Aldren A. Watson (New York: Dover Publications, 1996); *ABC of Bookbinding: A Unique Glossary With Over 700 Illustrations for Collectors & Librarians*, by Jane Greenfield (New Castle, Del.: Oak Knoll Books, 2002); *The Care of Fine Books*, by Jane Greenfield (New York: Skyhorse Publishing, 2007); and *The Encyclopedia of Papermaking and Bookbinding*, by Heidi Reimer-Epp and Mary Reimer (Philadelphia: Running Press Book Publishers, 2002) for the history of different styles of bookbinding and definitions of terms used in the field.

Contact the conservation or preservation department at your local library. The department may offer tours of its facilities or workshops on the proper care of books. Contact professional librarian associations; they may have divisions devoted to conservation. Community colleges and art museums often have weekend or evening classes in the conservation and book arts.

Finally, you might try contacting your local park district or community center to suggest sessions about book conservation. Many such groups offer summer day camps or after-school programs and look for input from participants about what types of activities are of interest. Plus, if you have had some conservation experience of your own, you could offer to teach younger students about how they can begin conserving books by taking good care of their own materials and the books they check out of the library.

EMPLOYERS

College and university libraries, public libraries, institutional libraries, and special libraries all employ book conservators. These organizations may have an entire department devoted to the conservation and preservation of materials, or the tasks of conservation may be bestowed upon another division, such as an archival or rare book collection. Museums sometimes have a specific book conservator post, or they may offer such duties to an interested art conservationist. Book conservators also work for companies devoted to material conservation. Binderies may hire a conservationist as a quality control consultant.

A number of book conservators are self-employed, working on a freelance or part-time basis for organizations and private citizens. They may be part of a nationwide network of certified book conservators. Often, potential clients contact book conservators through membership in professional organizations.

STARTING OUT

Book conservation is a field that relies heavily on skill, reputation, and word-of-mouth communication. While earning your bachelor's or master's degree, you should try to get an internship, apprenticeship, or assistantship in conservation or a related field. Take all the courses you can that will help you gain conservation skills.

You may also be able to get a part-time or summer job in your school library's preservation or conservation department. Many part-time positions or internships can turn into full-time jobs after the incumbent has proven his or her skills or completed specific educational requirements.

Once you complete a training period, you might consider becoming certified. Certification can be a deciding factor in gaining employment, since certain companies and organizations may require book conservators to have official affirmation of their qualifications from an outside agency.

You should also join a conservators' organization in order to get to know professionals in the field. Since many conservator positions are in libraries, you may wish to join a professional library association as well. Professional organizations often have job listings available to members. They also publish journals and newsletters to keep members up-to-date on new developments in the field.

If you are looking to be a self-employed conservator, you may wish to volunteer your services until you have established yourself. Volunteering to assist nonprofit organizations with their conservation needs will give you good exposure to help you learn more about the book conservator world and the skills that potential clients are seeking.

ADVANCEMENT

Book conservators who demonstrate a high level of skill in their craft can move on to positions with more responsibility. They may be called upon to train assistants in book conservation or to teach conservation techniques at a library school, certification program, or conservation lab.

They may also transfer their skill in dealing with rare and fine materials and work more in the art community as art conservators, appraisers, or artists. With more experience and education, a book conservator can become an archivist, curator, or librarian. Many book conservators prefer to move away from full-time conservation and work on freelance projects instead.

With advanced computer knowledge, book conservators can help bring rare and fragile materials into the digital age. They may learn how to make materials available on the Internet and become virtual curators. They may also move on to actual exhibition work. Understanding how to preserve materials gives them the advantage in knowing how to exhibit them safely.

As book conservators gain more prominent positions, the trend is away from materials and toward administration. Beginning conservators will often spend most of their day dealing directly with the materials to be conserved. Conservators who move on to more advanced positions generally spend more time training others; evaluating materials and methods; dealing with outside suppliers, customers, and associations; attending meetings; and planning for the future of the department and the field.

EARNINGS

It is difficult to say how much the average book conservator makes, since many conservators work part time, are self-employed, or have positions that encompass other duties as well. In general, the salary range for book conservators may fall within the range the U.S.

Department of Labor reports for museum conservators and technicians. In 2009, this group of professionals had a median annual income of $37,120. The lowest paid 10 percent earned less than $23,530 yearly, and the highest paid 10 percent made more than $67,090 per year. Often the size of the employer affects how much a conservator earns, with larger employers able to pay more. In addition, book conservators in major metropolitan areas generally earn more than those in small cities, and those with greater skills also command higher salaries.

Conservators who work for libraries, conservation organizations, large corporations, institutions, or government agencies generally receive a full range of benefits, including health care coverage, vacation days, paid holidays, paid sick time, and retirement savings plans. Self-employed book conservators usually have to provide their own benefits. All conservators have the added benefit of working with rare and unique materials. They have the opportunity to work with history and preserve an artifact for the future.

WORK ENVIRONMENT

Because of the damage that dirt, humidity, and the sun can cause to books, most conservators work in clean, climate-controlled areas away from direct sunlight. Many conservation labs are small offices, which often employ the conservator alone or perhaps with one or two part-time assistants. Other labs are part of a larger department within an organization; the University of Chicago's Regenstein Library, for instance, has a conservation lab within the Special Collections Research Center. With this type of arrangement, the book conservator generally has a few student and non-student assistants who work part time to help with some of the conservation duties.

Book conservators are always on the move. They use their hands constantly to measure, cut, and paste materials. They also bend, lift, and twist in order to reach items they work on and make room for new materials. Also, books are not always an easy size or weight to handle. Some oversized items need to be transported on a book truck from the stack area to the conservation area for treatment.

Most book conservators work 40 hours a week, usually during regular, weekday working hours. Depending on the needs of their department and the clientele they serve, book conservators may need to be available some weekend hours. Also, some book conservators may agree to travel to the homes of clients to view materials that may require conservation.

OUTLOOK

Employment for all conservators is expected to grow much faster than the average for all careers through 2018, according to the U.S. Department of Labor. Opportunities in book conservation will not be as strong, since book conservation is a small field and there is strong competition for jobs. Book conservators who are graduates of conservation programs and are willing to relocate should have the best opportunities for employment. Those who can use their conservation skills in tandem with other abilities may also find more job openings. Book conservators with an artistic bent, for instance, could bring their conservation skills to an exhibition program at an art museum. Conservators who enjoy public contact could use their practical experience to teach classes in conservation techniques.

Some people are concerned that our increasingly digital society will create fewer opportunities for book conservators. They claim that new technologies such as e-books, television, computers, telephones, and the Internet have changed communication styles so drastically that printed books will eventually become obsolete. While it is true that more advanced technology will bring new challenges to conservation, these advances should also increase opportunities for conservators who can blend these developments with traditional conservation efforts. For example, a book conservator with excellent computer skills and Web-authoring knowledge can work on a project to digitize rare book collections and make them available to people all over the world.

FOR MORE INFORMATION

For certification information, contact
 Academy of Certified Archivists
 1450 Western Avenue, Suite 101
 Albany, NY 12203-3539
 Tel: 518-694-8471
 http://www.certifiedarchivists.org

For information about how to become a conservator, contact
 American Institute for Conservation of Historic and Artistic
   Works
 1156 15th Street, NW, Suite 320
 Washington DC 20005-1714
 Tel: 202-452-9545
 E-mail: info@conservation-us.org
 http://www.conservation-us.org

For information on book conservation, contact
Guild of Book Workers
521 Fifth Avenue
New York, NY 10175-0038
http://www.guildofbookworkers.org

For information about preservation methods, services, and opportunities, contact
Library of Congress Preservation Directorate
101 Independence Avenue, SE
Washington, DC 20540-4500
Tel: 202-707-5213
http://lcweb.loc.gov/preserv

For information on conservation opportunities in Canada, contact
Canadian Conservation Institute
15 Eddy Street
Gatineau, Quebec K1A 0M5 Canada
Tel: 866-811-0055
E-mail: info@pch.gc.ca
http://www.pch.gc.ca/cci-icc

For a wealth of information about conservation topics, visit
Conservation OnLine
http://cool.conservation-us.org

Cataloging Librarians

QUICK FACTS

School Subjects
Computer science
English

Personal Skills
Communication/ideas
Helping/teaching

Work Environment
Primarily indoors
Primarily one location

Minimum Education Level
Master's degree

Salary Range
$33,480 to $53,710 to
$82,450+

Certification or Licensing
None available

Outlook
About as fast as the average

DOT
100

GOE
12.03.04

NOC
5111

O*NET-SOC
25-4021.00

OVERVIEW

Cataloging librarians, also known as *library catalogers*, classify newly acquired items such as books, magazines, DVDs, music CDs, and digitized materials for online collections in a standardized way in order to give patrons easy access to the materials. They organize and cross reference materials according to title, author, date published, subject matter, or a keyword, and publish this information in an online public access catalog. Cataloging librarians work in public libraries, schools, universities and colleges, special libraries, and museums. Many cataloging librarians belong to the American Library Association, an organization dedicated to the promotion and improvement of library services and the librarianship profession. Approximately 159,900 librarians are employed throughout the United States. Cataloging librarians make up a small percentage of this group.

HISTORY

Libraries have existed since around 3000 B.C. Ancient Sumerian libraries contained clay tablets with cuneiform inscriptions (written with a stylus) baked onto them, and Egyptian libraries housed hieroglyphic accounts recorded on papyrus rolls. Early catalogers summarized the contents of these clay tablets and papyrus rolls so that users could search them quickly.

The mass production of books began in the 1400s, with the invention of movable metal type by Johannes Gutenberg. As more books were printed and libraries grew in size, it quickly became clear that someone was needed to classify the books so that they could be

easily accessed by the books' owners. Cataloging librarians classified books by a variety of methods—color, size, title, author, subject
matter, and the name of the person who donated the book. These
methods could be very confusing, as there was no set standard from
library to library or librarian to librarian.

Many cite Antonio Panizzi, an Italian expatriate lawyer who
worked at the British Museum, as the father of modern cataloging.
When he began working at the museum in 1831, he found it, according to Michael Gorman in *American Libraries*, a "disorganized and
random collection of books cataloged by indigent clergymen and
other part-time drudges." The collection was only partly cataloged,
and was organized by a confusing classification system that made
it difficult to locate titles. In 1836, Panizzi suggested that an author
catalog with a subject index should be used instead of a classed catalog. Around this time, he and several other librarians wrote *Rules
for the Compilation of the Catalogue*, which is still referenced today
by modern catalogers.

Although *Rules for the Compilation of the Catalogue* advanced
the field of cataloging, there was still great debate about how to catalog books and other materials. In 1908, the American Library Association and the Library Association of the United Kingdom published

Ten Largest U.S. Libraries

Institution	Volumes Held
1. Library of Congress	32,818,014
2. Boston Public Library	23,595,895
3. Harvard University	16,250,117
4. New York Public Library	15,348,427
5. Yale University	12,519,514
6. University of Illinois–Urbana-Champaign	11,686,060
7. University of California–Berkeley	11,087,687
8. Columbia University	10,296,816
9. University of Texas–Austin	9,447,434
10. Public Library of Cincinnati and Hamilton County	9,261,259

Source: American Library Association

a set of common cataloging rules. This marked the beginning of a trend toward the internationalization and standardization of library cataloging. In the past century, many rules have been established that help cataloging librarians do their jobs more efficiently.

Today, technology has changed the way cataloging librarians do their work. Instead of card files, they now use computerized database retrieval systems. In addition to classifying printed books, they also classify e-books, CD-ROMs, videos, DVDs, and any other materials that modern libraries offer to patrons.

THE JOB

Imagine going to a library to do research for an upcoming class report. How can you find out if there are any books pertaining to your topic? Where are these resources kept? Are there any other materials (such as DVDs) to consider when doing the research? Thanks to the work of cataloging librarians, there is a systematic approach to the way library resources are recorded, cross-referenced, and organized.

Cataloging librarians are responsible for creating a record for all new items acquired by the library. These items include books, magazines, DVDs, music CDs, and digitized materials for online collections. They describe each item following a standard set of rules (usually AACR2, Anglo-American Cataloging Rules, 2nd revised edition) and put the information in a standard computerized format. This information includes title, subject matter, date of publication, the material's format, and the author's name. They may also write a short description, or summary, of the item. For example, if a book is about the country of Italy, the cataloging librarian would create a short write-up that details the type of information presented in the book—such as the history of the country, travel destinations, or its culinary offerings. Finally, the cataloging librarian assigns a classification number, or call number, for the item. This call number is a unique number used for the purpose of identification, but also as a way to keep the shelving process organized. For example, a children's joke book may be assigned a call number of j398.6, if a patron goes to that particular shelf, 398, she would then find other joke books.

Cataloging librarians must make many decisions when classifying books. For example, when working with new fiction written by A. N. Roquelaure, the cataloger would make the decision whether to cross-reference the books with the author's real name, Anne Rice. Another example of a cataloging decision would be how to list a set of travel guides. How should a boxed set of travel DVDs be classified? Individually by country, or as a set?

Sometimes, libraries acquire items that are too bulky, or documents too valuable, to shelve. In such cases, cataloging librarians may photograph the item, and assign a code. This way, patrons may still be made aware such items are within the library, and their location.

Cataloging librarians may create different catalogs for specific audiences, such as children. They may include simple summaries and even graphics to make profiles attractive and easy to understand. In the past, cataloging librarians put information into a card catalog, a collection of small cards alphabetized according to title, subject matter, or by the author's name. Today, cataloging is done in online databases, which makes creating, organizing, and finding the records for materials much easier for the library's staff and its patrons. Online databases also allow several libraries to share their resources, as well as determine if they already have many copies of the same book or other items. Currently, many libraries follow AACR2, which gives a specific guideline on how to construct and maintain catalog records. However, many libraries are expected to convert from the AACR2 system to the Resource Description and Access (RDA) system. Proponents of the RDA system believe that it will be easier to use internationally and allow for more flexibility when describing nonbook materials such as online resources, music, and images.

Cataloging librarians not only work in public libraries, but academic libraries, and the libraries of museums, large corporations, or for special archives. Those working in such settings may have additional responsibilities such as reviewing or revising cataloging policies, database management, or cataloging statistics for departmental reports. Cataloging librarians may be responsible for the management and training of assistant catalogers, graduate interns, or volunteers.

REQUIREMENTS

High School
In high school, take a college preparatory course load. Suggested courses include history, English, computer science, and speech. Also, most cataloging librarians have a reading knowledge of at least one foreign language, so it is a good idea to begin foreign language classes while in high school.

Postsecondary Training
A strong undergraduate liberal arts education will prepare you well for graduate study in library science. Many library schools don't

require specific undergraduate courses for acceptance, but a good academic record and reading knowledge of at least one foreign language is usually required. Classes that strengthen your communication, writing, and research skills will also be useful.

You will need to earn a master's degree to become a librarian. The degree is generally known as the master of library science (M.L.S.), but in some institutions it may be referred to by a different title, such as the master of library and information science (M.L.I.S.). You should plan to attend a graduate school of library and information science that is accredited by the American Library Association (ALA). Currently, there are nearly 50 ALA-accredited schools. Some libraries do not consider job applicants who attended a nonaccredited school. Visit http://www.ala.org/ala/educationcareers/education/accreditedprograms/directory for a list of ALA-accredited programs.

If you plan to work as a cataloging librarian in a special library, such as a law, music, or medical library, you must have a very strong background in that subject. Most special cataloging librarians have a degree in their subject specialization in addition to their M.L.S.

Other Requirements

Cataloging librarians must have analytical minds and a methodical approach to their work. They should enjoy sorting and organizing materials, be able to work well alone and with others, and be able to quickly skim materials in order to determine how they should be classified. They should enjoy conducting research and have a love of books and other library resources. Strong oral communication skills are important since cataloging librarians must interact effectively with managers and coworkers. Finally, strong computer and technology skills, as well as a willingness to continue to learn throughout one's careers, are key to success in this field.

EXPLORING

You can learn more about the work of librarians by volunteering in your school or local library, reading books and magazines about the field, and participating in school library clubs. You can also talk to your school or local librarian about career options (including those in cataloging) or ask a career counselor to arrange an information interview with a cataloging librarian.

The ALA provides a wealth of career information at its Web site, LibraryCareers.org (http://www.ala.org/ala/educationcareers/careers/librarycareerssite/home.cfm). Visit the Web sites of the ALA and other library science organizations to learn more about the field. You can also visit the Web sites of accredited library science programs to learn more about typical classes, degree requirements, and other aspects of library science.

EMPLOYERS

Approximately 159,900 librarians are employed in the United States. Cataloging librarians make up a small percentage of this total. Cataloging librarians work in academic, public, special, and government libraries. Opportunities are available throughout the United States, but are most frequently found in large cities and urban areas.

STARTING OUT

While still in college, you may be able to learn about job opportunities via your school's career services office. Library internships and volunteer positions will also provide you with networking contacts that may be of use to you during your job search.

Most professional library and information science organizations have job listings that candidates can consult. The ALA job Web site, http://joblist.ala.org, for example, offers links to employment opportunities throughout the country, as posted by different library organizations. The ALA also offers a career guidance Web site, http://www.getajob.ala.org, that provides tips on landing a job. Other useful library-related job-search and career resource sites include LisJobs.com (http://lisjobs.com) and Library Job Postings on the Internet (http://www.libraryjobpostings.org).

ADVANCEMENT

Cataloging librarians with advanced education and experience can become library managers or directors. They may find employment with a larger library or teach at a college or university. A doctorate is desirable for reaching top administrative levels, as well as for taking a graduate library school faculty position. Some cataloging librarians may become archivists or catalogers at museums or cultural centers.

EARNINGS

Salaries for librarians vary by the location, size, and type of library, the amount of experience the librarian has, and the responsibilities of the position. The U.S. Department of Labor (DOL) does not provide salary information for cataloging librarians. It does report that median annual earnings for all librarians were $53,710 in 2009. Salaries ranged from less than $33,480 to more than $82,450. Librarians working in colleges and universities had mean annual earnings of $59,430. Librarians employed in local government earned $49,920, while those who worked for the federal government earned $79,550.

Most librarians receive a full benefits package, which may include paid sick leave, vacation time, retirement savings programs, and various insurance plans.

WORK ENVIRONMENT

Most libraries are pleasant and comfortable places to work. Cataloging librarians do not typically work with the public, but rather in private offices or cubicles. They often work alone or in small groups of catalogers. Most cataloging librarians work a standard 35- to 40-hour workweek. Cataloging librarians who work at large libraries that acquire a large volume of new materials that need to be cataloged may occasionally face demanding and stressful work conditions. They also may suffer eyestrain and headaches from working long hours at the computer.

OUTLOOK

Employment for librarians is expected to grow about as fast as the average for all careers through 2018, according to the DOL. An expected wave of retirements in the next decade will create opportunities for aspiring librarians. Cataloging is also becoming a more in-demand specialty as a result of the increasing types of media that need to be cataloged and technological advances that allow library patrons to search for items from home or other nonlibrary settings.

FOR MORE INFORMATION

For information on careers in law librarianship, contact
American Association of Law Libraries
105 West Adams Street, Suite 3300
Chicago, IL 60603-6225
Tel: 312-939-4764
http://www.aallnet.org

For a list of accredited schools and information on careers, scholarships and grants, and membership, contact
American Library Association
50 East Huron Street

Chicago, IL 60611-2729
Tel: 800-545-2433
http://www.ala.org

To *learn more about information science careers, contact*
American Society for Information Science and Technology
1320 Fenwick Lane, Suite 510
Silver Spring, MD 20910-3560
Tel: 301-495-0900
E-mail: asis@asis.org
http://www.asis.org

For more information on careers, contact
Association for Library Collections and Technical Services
50 East Huron Street
Chicago, IL 60611-2795
Tel: 800-545-2433, ext. 5037
E-mail: alcts@ala.org
http://www.ala.org/ala/mgrps/divs/alcts

For information on employment in academic settings, contact
Association of College and Research Libraries
c/o American Library Association
50 East Huron Street
Chicago, IL 60611-2795
Tel: 800-545-2433, ext. 2523
E-mail: acrl@ala.org
http://www.ala.org/ala/mgrps/divs/acrl

For information on employment in research settings, contact
Association of Research Libraries
21 Dupont Circle, NW, Suite 800
Washington DC 20036-1543
Tel: 202-296-2296
http://www.arl.org

For information on careers in medical librarianship, contact
Medical Library Association
65 East Wacker Place, Suite 1900
Chicago, IL 60601-7246
Tel: 312-419-9094
E-mail: info@mlahq.org
http://www.mlanet.org

For information on careers in music librarianship, contact
Music Library Association
8551 Research Way, Suite 180
Middleton, WI 53562-3567
Tel: 608-836-5825
E-mail: mla@areditions.com
http://www.musiclibraryassoc.org

To read Careers in Public Librarianship, *visit*
Public Library Association
c/o American Library Association
50 East Huron Street
Chicago, IL 60611-2795
Tel: 800-545-2433, ext. 5752
http://www.ala.org/ala/mgrps/divs/pla

For information on working in a specialized library, contact
Special Libraries Association
331 South Patrick Street
Alexandria, VA 22314-3501
Tel: 703-647-4900
http://www.sla.org

For information on the field of competitive intelligence, contact
Strategic and Competitive Intelligence Professionals
1700 Diagonal Road, Suite 600
Alexandria, VA 22314-2863
Tel: 703-739-0696
E-mail: info@scip.org
http://www.scip.org

To receive information on librarianship in Canada, contact
Canadian Library Association
1150 Morrison Drive, Suite 400
Ottawa, ON K2H 8S9 Canada
Tel: 613-232-9625
E-mail: info@cla.ca
http://www.cla.ca

Children's Librarians

OVERVIEW

Children's librarians oversee the daily operations of the children's department of public and private libraries and school libraries. They purchase books, periodicals, music and films, and other informational material, and prepare them for circulation. Children's librarians also serve as instructors and mentors to students. In addition, they conduct activities to introduce children to different types of literature. These activities include story time, reading challenges, book discussions, and outreach projects. Approximately 159,900 librarians (including children's librarians) are employed in the United States.

HISTORY

Since ancient times, libraries have been centers where adults could learn, read, and access information. But until the 19th century, no libraries devoted sections to the specific needs and interests of children.

Library historians disagree on when the first public library in the United States that featured resources for children was founded. In 1837, the Arlington (Massachusetts) Public Library became one of the first libraries to offer access to children, according to *The World Wide School*, by Alice Hazeltine. Families could check out as many as three books and keep them for 30 days. They were even allowed to pull books from the shelves until a change in the library's charter stated that "no person except the librarian shall remove a book from the shelves."

During the 1830s, school district libraries also began to appear in New York and New England and eventually spread throughout the country. Materials in these libraries were typically geared toward assisting students write papers and study for tests.

By the late 1890s and early 1900s, public libraries with children's sections were founded in several major U.S. cities. The Children's Librarian Section of the American Library Association was founded in 1901 to support this new library specialty. During these years, school districts and individual schools also continued to improve their library services. The American Association of School Librarians was founded in 1951, but traces its origins to the early 1910s via various children-oriented discussion groups and roundtables facilitated by its parent organization, the American Library Association.

Today, children's libraries feature not only books, but also periodicals, DVDs, films, audio recordings, maps, photographs, music, toys, games, puzzles, and a variety of other useful resources for children. They work with both electronic and printed materials.

THE JOB

Many libraries have special departments that cater to children. This library within a library, often called a children's library, houses collections of age-appropriate fiction and nonfiction, as well as research tools such as encyclopedias and atlases. They may also have computers that feature programs and games that appeal to the young and more traditional toys and puzzles. Oftentimes, librarians choose to work with a particular age group. Those who work specifically with children and young adults are referred to as children's librarians or *youth services librarians*. If employed in a school setting, such librarians are called *library media specialists*. Regardless of title, children's librarians help young library patrons find and select information best suited to their needs, whether for school research, personal knowledge, or simply the enjoyment of reading a book or finding a useful or entertaining resource.

Maintaining and organizing library facilities are the primary responsibilities of children's librarians. One major task is selecting and ordering books and other media, including fiction and nonfiction, reference books such as encyclopedias and dictionaries, study guides, maps, periodicals, videos, DVDs, and music. These materials must be organized so library patrons can access them easily. New acquisitions are cataloged by title, author, and subject matter. Today, cataloging is computerized. Each book is given a label and card pocket, and stamped with the library's name and address. A bar code is attached to help keep track of its location. Children's librarians must regularly inventory their collection to locate lost or overdue books, identify books that need repairs, or to dispose of outdated or worn materials.

Libraries are given an annual budget by either the school board or library board. Children's librarians must consider this budget when making new purchases or additions to the collection. When the budget allows, they fulfill special book requests from children, teachers, or parents.

Children's librarians are teachers as well. They have a thorough knowledge of their library's collection so they can effectively help students with any research questions, or guide them toward a reading selection suited for their grade or reading level. They are familiar with the works of established authors, as well as newly published books and series. Children's librarians also teach effective ways to navigate library resources using the Dewey Decimal System, online catalog systems, or research on the Internet. They work with area schools and teachers to help plan and organize upcoming class projects and tests. Many times, they provide instruction to patrons and students on the use of library equipment—computers, audiovisual equipment, copy machines, or computer programs.

The implementation of special projects is also a major responsibility of children's librarians. They host story time for toddlers and preschool-age children, often planning a special craft project related to the day's story. Children's librarians often schedule holiday parties and puppet shows. They may offer school-age children summer reading programs and challenges, author visits, or book clubs.

Children's librarians also organize displays of books, artwork, collections, or memorabilia that may be of interest to children. They are responsible for soliciting the display of private collections and setting up and dismantling the displays. They create a comfortable and inviting space that is appealing to children of all ages using colorful furniture and cozy reading areas. They also decorate the library with book displays, posters, toys, and seasonal items.

Children's librarians are also responsible for outreach services such as the bookmobile. These mini-libraries house a collection of books and periodicals that travel to different locations in the community. Library employees staff the book mobile and often conduct a story and craft time for the children. Children's librarians may also promote library services at area preschools via storytelling, book totes, and bookmarks.

Children's librarians also have management duties. They supervise library technicians and nonprofessional staff such as clerks, student workers, or volunteers. They often train staff regarding the layout of the library, use of special equipment, or new computer programs.

A librarian reads a book to two first graders. *(Bob Daemmrich, The Image Works)*

REQUIREMENTS

High School

A full academic course load—including history, math, English, speech, and computer science—is your best preparation for a career as a children's librarian. Familiarity with the Dewey Decimal System is important so you can navigate your way around a library. Also, join clubs or find activities that will give you plenty of experience playing and working with children. Some examples include taking child development courses in high school, babysitting neighborhood children, or volunteering at a summer camp or after-school program for kids.

Postsecondary Training

A master's degree in library science from an accredited school is required for most children's librarian positions in public libraries. Library Management, Youth Services Librarianship, Literature and Resources Children, and History of Children's Literature are just some of the typical courses that students take for this degree. Workshops covering topics such as electronic publishing and library materials and services for very young children are offered to complement more traditional educational programs.

Those employed in a school setting can take a different route to this career. Some schools require their librarians to hold teacher certification before receiving training or certification in library science. Requirements differ by state.

Certification or Licensing

Children's librarians in some states may be required to earn teacher certification and/or a master's degree in addition to preparation as a librarian. Education and certification requirements vary by state, county, and local governments. Contact the school board or public library system in your area to learn about specific requirements. You can check your state's requirements at Web sites such as the University of Kentucky College of Education's Web page, http://www.uky .edu/Education/TEP/usacert.html. The site provides links to teaching certification requirements for each state, which is especially helpful if you plan on working as a children's librarian in another state during your career.

Other Requirements

Children's librarians should enjoy working with children. They must be good teachers and have the patience to explain library services and technology to children of varying ages and levels of understanding. Children's librarians should also have strong interpersonal skills, the ability to solve problems, and be detail oriented. They must also love information and be committed to pursuing continuing education throughout their careers.

EXPLORING

Volunteering to work in your school library is an excellent way to learn more about this career. Many schools rely on students to assist school librarians. As a media center aide, you may be asked to staff the library checkout desk, shelve returned books and periodicals, or maintain audiovisual equipment. Volunteering or working part time at your local library is the ideal way to explore this career. You can get hands-on experience with the working routine of a real library and network for future job opportunities.

Don't forget to visit Web sites of library associations such as the American Library Association, the Association for Library Service to Children, and the American Association of School Librarians. Their sites can provide a wealth of information about education programs, scholarships, financial aid, certification, and membership.

EMPLOYERS

Approximately 159,900 librarians are employed in the United States. Children's librarians work for public and private libraries and elementary and secondary schools.

STARTING OUT

To break into this career, turn to library association Web sites or publications for job listings and recruiters. Your college's career services office can also provide job leads. The ALA job Web site, http://joblist.ala.org, for example, offers links to employment opportunities throughout the country, as posted by different library organizations. The ALA also offers a career guidance Web site, http://www.getajob.ala.org, that provides tips on landing a job.

ADVANCEMENT

Experienced children's librarians may advance by taking a position in a larger school district or in a larger library system. Others, with additional education, may become library directors or library educators.

Some children's librarians pursue careers in other fields. Children's author Beverly Cleary and former first lady Laura Bush are two examples of famous former children's librarians. Others may use their experience in the field to work as consultants to publishing companies.

EARNINGS

Salaries for children's librarians depend on such factors as the size, location, and type of library; the responsibilities of the position; and the amount of experience the librarian has. According to the U.S. Department of Labor (DOL), median annual earnings of librarians in were $53,710 in 2009. Ten percent of all librarians earned less than $33,480, and 10 percent earned $82,450 or more annually. Librarians working in elementary and secondary schools earned a mean annual salary of $57,950 in 2009. Librarians employed by local government earned a mean annual salary of $49,920 in 2009.

Most librarians receive compensated sick leave, paid vacation time, holiday pay, various insurance plans, and retirement savings programs.

WORK ENVIRONMENT

Most children's librarians work a 40-hour week, with hours scheduled depending on the operational time of the main library or school. Some librarians prefer to work part time. The work environment, whether at a library or school, is comfortable and pleasant. Libraries, especially those designated for children, are usually colorfully decorated with many workspaces and cozy reading nooks. Most libraries are open from early in the morning until evening, and keep weekend hours as well. Librarians employed in a school setting usually have the same work hours as teachers and receive time off during summer and spring breaks and teacher institute days. Library media specialists report directly to the principal of their school; those employed at a public library report to the library director.

OUTLOOK

The DOL predicts that employment for librarians, including children's librarians, will grow about as fast as the average for all careers through 2018. This specialty is a popular choice for many aspiring librarians, which means that competition for the best jobs will remain strong over the next decade. Children's librarians who are willing to relocate or take lesser paying positions in rural areas will have the best employment prospects.

FOR MORE INFORMATION

For career information and a list of accredited educational programs, contact
American Association of School Librarians
c/o American Library Association
50 East Huron Street
Chicago, IL 60611-2795
Tel: 800-545-2433, ext. 4382
E-mail: aasl@ala.org
http://www.ala.org/ala/mgrps/divs/aasl

For a list of accredited schools and information on careers, scholarships and grants, and membership, contact
American Library Association
50 East Huron Street
Chicago, IL 60611-2729
Tel: 800-545-2433
http://www.ala.org

For information on a career as a children's librarian, contact
Association for Library Service to Children
c/o American Library Association
50 East Huron Street
Chicago, IL 60611-2795
Tel: 800-545-2433, ext. 2163
E-mail: alsc@ala.org
http://www.ala.org/ala/mgrps/divs/alsc

For career information about librarians who provide services to students ages 12–18, visit
Young Adult Library Services Association
c/o American Library Association
50 East Huron Street
Chicago, IL 60611-2795
Tel: 800-545-2433, ext. 4390
E-mail: YALSA@ala.org
http://www.ala.org/ala/mgrps/divs/yalsa/yalsa.cfm

College Professors, Library and Information Science

OVERVIEW

College professors, library and information science, also known as *library science educators*, instruct undergraduate and graduate students in library and information science at colleges and universities. They lecture classes, lead small seminar groups, and create and grade examinations. They also may conduct research, write for publication, and aid in administration. Approximately 3,940 library science educators are employed in the United States.

HISTORY

All early libraries were intended for the use of small, elite groups. The industrial revolution and other social changes in the 18th and 19th centuries upset the old social order, and new generations of working people were able to acquire an education. Their desires called for a new kind of library, one that not only would preserve the best works of earlier times but also would be an educational facility for the common people. To this end, associations of young mercantile workers, apprentices, mechanics, and clerks began to form libraries. In 1731, Benjamin Franklin and a group of his friends organized the Library Company of Philadelphia, the earliest library of this kind in the American colonies. The first public library, supported from public funds and open to all readers, was established in Boston in 1854. By 1876, there were 342 public libraries in the United States.

College Library Treasures

College libraries are repositories for rare, and occasionally off-beat, collections. Consider the collections of some of the following colleges:

- Surfing Collection at San Diego State University (http://scua .sdsu.edu/collections/surfing.shtml)
- Jane Austen Collection at Goucher College (http://www.goucher .edu/x10707.xml)
- Albert H. Small Declaration of Independence Collection at the University of Virginia (http://www2.lib.virginia.edu/ small/collections/small)
- J.R.R. Tolkien Collection at Marquette University (http://www .marquette.edu/library/archives/tolkien.shtml)
- Nietz Old Textbook Collection at the University of Pittsburgh (http://digital.library.pitt.edu/nietz/biblio/search.html)
- Japanese Americans Interned in Arkansas Collection at the University of Arkansas (http://libinfo.uark.edu/specialcollections/ research/guides/japaneseamericans.asp)
- Fox Film Corporation Publicity Photographs Collection at the University of Tennessee (http://dlc.lib.utk.edu/f/fa/fulltext/2371 .html)
- Flannery O'Connor Collection at Georgia College & State University (http://www.gcsu.edu/library/sc/collections/oconnor/ foccoll.htm)
- Early Comic Strips, 1898–1916 Collection at Duke University (http://library.duke.edu/exhibits/earlycomicstrips)

Despite the steady growth of public and private libraries in the United States, it was not until 1887 that the first library school—the School of Library Economy—was established at Columbia University in New York by Melvil Dewey, the originator of the Dewey Decimal System. Until that time, librarians received their training through an apprenticeship at a library or by taking classes, formal training, or some other type of instruction at a university library.

The Association of American Library Schools was founded in 1915 to represent the interests and professional concerns of library educators. Today, it is known as the Association for Library and Information Science Education.

In 1926, the first graduate library school was established at the University of Chicago. The university also offered the first doctoral program in library studies.

Today, there are nearly 50 master's programs in library and information studies accredited by the American Library Association, as well as hundreds of programs that offer certificate, associate's, and bachelor's degrees in library and information science.

As the field of information science becomes more complex due to technological innovations and specialization, library science educators will continue to be in demand to teach tomorrow's librarians and information professionals.

THE JOB

College and university library science educators teach at junior colleges or at four-year colleges and universities. At four-year institutions, most faculty members are assistant professors, associate professors, or full professors. These three types of professorships differ in regards to status, job responsibilities, and salary. Assistant professors are new faculty members who are working to get tenure (status as a permanent professor); they seek to advance to associate and then to full professorships.

Library science professors perform three main functions: teaching, service, and research and publication. Their most important responsibility is to teach students. Their role within a college department will determine the level of courses they teach and the number of courses per semester. Professors may head several classes a semester or only a few each year. Some of their classes will have large enrollment, while graduate seminars may consist of only 12 or fewer students. Though library science educators may spend only 12 to 16 hours a week in the actual classroom, they spend many hours preparing lectures and lesson plans, grading papers and exams, and preparing grade reports. They also schedule office hours during the week to be available to students outside of the lecture hall, and they meet with students individually throughout the semester. In the classroom, library science educators lecture, lead discussions, administer exams, and assign textbook reading and other research.

An important part of teaching is advising students. Not all library science faculty members serve as advisers, but those who do must set aside large blocks of time to guide students through the program. Library science educators who serve as advisers may have any number of students assigned to them, from fewer than 10 to more than 100, depending on the administrative policies of the college. Their responsibility may involve looking over a planned program of studies to make sure the students meet requirements for graduation, or it may involve working intensively with each student on many aspects of college life.

All college professors provide important services to their department, college, or profession. Many college professors edit technical journals, review research and scholarship, and head committees about their field of expertise. College professors also serve on committees that determine the curriculum or make decisions about student learning.

The third responsibility of library science faculty members is research and publication. Faculty members who are heavily involved in research programs sometimes are assigned a smaller teaching load. Library science educators publish their research findings in various scholarly journals. They also write books based on their research or on their own knowledge and experience in the field. Most textbooks are written by college and university teachers.

Some library science educators eventually rise to the position of *department chair*, where they govern the affairs of the entire library and information science department. Library science department chairs, faculty, and other professional staff members are aided in their myriad duties by *graduate assistants*, who may help develop teaching materials, conduct research, give examinations, teach lower-level courses, and carry out other activities.

Distance learning programs, an increasingly popular option for students, give library science professors the opportunity to use today's technologies to remain in one place while teaching students who are at a variety of locations simultaneously. (To view a good example of an online library science program, visit http://www.lis .illinois.edu/academics/leep.) The professor's duties, like those when teaching correspondence courses conducted by mail, include grading work that students send in at periodic intervals and advising students of their progress. Computers, the Internet, e-mail, and video conferencing, however, are some of the technology tools that allow library science professors and students to communicate in "real time" in a virtual classroom setting. Meetings may be scheduled during the same time as traditional classes or during evenings and weekends. Library science professors who do this work are sometimes known as *extension work, correspondence,* or *distance learning instructors.* They may teach online courses in addition to other classes or may have distance learning as their major teaching responsibility.

The *junior college library and information science instructor* has many of the same kinds of responsibilities as does the teacher in a four-year college or university. Because junior colleges offer only a two-year program, they teach only undergraduates.

REQUIREMENTS

High School

Your high school's college preparatory program likely includes courses in English, science, foreign language, history, math, and government. In addition, you should take courses in speech to get a sense of what it will be like to lecture to a group of students. Your school's debate team can also help you develop public speaking skills, along with research skills.

Postsecondary Training

At least one advanced degree in library and information science is required to be a library science professor in a college or university. The master's degree is considered the minimum standard, and graduate work beyond the master's is usually desirable. If you hope to advance in academic rank above instructor, most institutions require a doctorate. In 2003, 90.5 percent of library science educators teaching at the graduate level had a doctoral degree, according to the Association for Library and Information Science Education.

In the last year of your undergraduate program, you'll apply to library and information science graduate programs. Standards for admission to library and information science graduate programs can be high and the competition heavy, depending on the school. Once accepted into a program, your responsibilities will be similar to those of your library science professors—in addition to attending seminars, you'll research, prepare articles for publication, and teach some undergraduate courses.

You may find employment in a junior college with only a master's degree. Advancement in responsibility and in salary, however, is more likely to come if you have earned a doctorate.

Other Requirements

You should enjoy reading, writing, and researching. Not only will you spend many years studying in school, but your whole career will be based on communicating your thoughts and ideas as well. People skills are important because you'll be dealing directly with students, administrators, and other faculty members on a daily basis. You should feel comfortable in a role of authority and possess self-confidence.

EXPLORING

Your high school teachers use many of the same skills as college professors, so talk to your teachers about their careers and their college experiences. You can develop your own teaching experience by volunteering at a community center, working at a day care center, or working at a summer camp. Also, spend some time on a college campus to get a sense of the environment. Contact colleges for their admissions brochures and course catalogs (or check them out online); read about the library science faculty members and the courses they teach. Before visiting college campuses, make arrangements to speak to professors who teach courses that interest you. These professors may allow you to sit in on their classes and observe. Also, make appointments with college advisers and with people in the admissions and recruitment offices. If your grades are good enough, you might be able to serve as a teaching assistant during your undergraduate years, which can give you experience leading discussions and grading papers.

EMPLOYERS

There are approximately 3,940 library science educators employed in the United States. Library science educators work for colleges and universities that have library science or information science programs. With a doctorate, a number of publications, and a record of good teaching, professors should find opportunities in universities all across the country. Library science professors teach in undergraduate and graduate programs. The teaching jobs at doctoral institutions are usually better paying and more prestigious. The most sought-after positions are those that offer tenure. Library science teachers who have only a master's degree will be limited to opportunities with junior colleges, community colleges, and some small private institutions.

STARTING OUT

You should start the process of finding a teaching position while you are in graduate school. The process includes developing a curriculum vitae (a detailed, academic resume), writing for publication, assisting with research, attending conferences, and gaining teaching experience and recommendations. Many students begin applying for teaching positions while finishing their graduate program. For most positions at four-year institutions, you must travel to large conferences where interviews can be arranged with representatives from the universities to which you have applied.

To learn more about potential employers, you should visit the American Library Association's Web site (http://www.ala.org) for a list of schools that have library science programs. You can also pick up a copy of the *Directory of LIS Programs and Faculty in the United States and Canada*, which is published by the Association for Library and Information Science Education. The association also offers job listings at its Web site, http://www.alise.org. Job listings can also be found in the *Chronicle of Higher Education* (http://chronicle.com).

Because of the competition for tenure-track positions, you may have to work for a few years in temporary positions, finding employment at various schools as an adjunct professor.

ADVANCEMENT

The normal pattern of advancement is from instructor to assistant professor, to associate professor, to full professor. All four academic ranks are concerned primarily with teaching and research. Library science educators who have an interest in and a talent for administration may be advanced to chair of their department or to dean of their college. A few become college or university presidents or other types of administrators.

The instructor is usually an inexperienced college teacher. He or she may hold a doctorate or may have completed all the Ph.D. requirements except for the dissertation. Most colleges look upon the rank of instructor as the period during which the college is trying out the teacher. Instructors usually are advanced to the position of assistant professors within three to four years. Assistant professors are given up to about six years to prove themselves worthy of tenure, and if they do so, they become associate professors. Some professors choose to remain at the associate level. Others strive to become full professors and receive greater status, salary, and responsibilities.

Most colleges have clearly defined promotion policies from rank to rank for faculty members, and many have written statements about the number of years in which instructors and assistant professors may remain in grade. Administrators in many colleges hope to encourage younger faculty members to increase their skills and competencies and thus to qualify for the more responsible positions of associate professor and full professor.

EARNINGS

Earnings vary by the size of the school, by the type of school (public, private, women's only, for example), and by the level of position the library science educator holds. According to the U.S. Department of Labor (DOL), in 2009, the median salary for library science educators was $60,650, with 10 percent earning $94,310 or more and 10 percent earning $39,440 or less. Those with the highest earnings tend to be senior tenured faculty; those with the lowest, graduate assistants. Professors working on the West Coast and the East Coast and those working at doctorate-granting institutions also tend to have the highest salaries. Many professors try to increase their earnings by completing research, publishing in their field, or teaching additional courses.

Benefits for full-time faculty typically include health insurance and retirement funds and, in some cases, stipends for travel related to research, housing allowances, and tuition waivers for dependents.

WORK ENVIRONMENT

A college or university is usually a pleasant place in which to work. Campuses bustle with all types of activities and events, stimulating ideas, and a young, energetic population. Much prestige comes with success as a library science professor and scholar; professors have the respect of students, colleagues, and others in their community.

Depending on the size of their department, library science educators may have their own office, or they may have to share an office with one or more colleagues. Their department may provide them with a computer, Internet access, and research assistants. Library science educators are also able to do much of their office work at home. They can arrange their schedule around class hours, academic meetings, and the established office hours when they meet with students. Most college teachers work more than 40 hours each week. Although library science educators may teach only two or three classes a semester, they spend many hours preparing for lectures, examining student work, and conducting research.

OUTLOOK

The DOL predicts faster than average employment growth for all college and university professors through 2018. College enrollment is projected to grow due to an increased number of 18- to 24-year-olds, an increased number of adults returning to college, and an increased number of foreign-born students. Opportunities for library science educators should also be strong over the next decade. Factors behind this prediction include an anticipated shortage of librarians during the next decade, a demand for more library science educators as existing educators retire, and continued growth in technology and information-gathering resources. However, competition for full-time, tenure-track positions at four-year schools will be very strong. Library science professionals with the highest education will have the best opportunities in coming years.

FOR MORE INFORMATION

To read about the issues affecting college professors, contact the following organizations:
American Association of University Professors
1133 19th Street, NW, Suite 200
Washington, DC 20036-3655
Tel: 202-737-5900
E-mail: aaup@aaup.org
http://www.aaup.org

American Federation of Teachers
555 New Jersey Avenue, NW
Washington, DC 20001-2029
Tel: 202-879-4400
http://www.aft.org

For a list of accredited schools and information on careers, scholarships and grants, and membership, contact
American Library Association
50 East Huron Street
Chicago, IL 60611-2729
Tel: 800-545-2433
http://www.ala.org

For information on careers in library science education, contact
Association for Library and Information Science Education
65 East Wacker Place, Suite 1900
Chicago, IL 60601-7246
Tel: 312-795-0996
E-mail: contact@alise.org
http://www.alise.org

Corporate Librarians

OVERVIEW

Corporate librarians manage data files and sources of information pertinent to the interest of a company, hospital, association, private business, or government department. They help company staff members with projects by conducting extensive research, writing reports, archiving data, or completing other tasks. Much of their work is Internet based. Corporate librarians also educate and train staff about new computer programs and databases. More than 8,900 special libraries are located throughout the United States. The Special Libraries Association (SLA) serves the interests of about 11,000 members internationally.

HISTORY

Although librarians have been employed by corporations and other businesses for decades, the career of corporate librarian did not really blossom until the emergence of computers, electronic databases, and the Internet during the past two decades. This new technology allowed companies to access and acquire huge amounts of information. But the information was useless unless it could be organized for ease of use. Companies turned to corporate librarians to sort, analyze, and organize this information. Today, corporate librarians are key members of businesses and are relied upon to effectively manage large amounts of information—which saves their employers valuable time and money.

THE JOB

Public libraries and schools are not the only place librarians can find employment. Today, many librarians work for various companies throughout the United States, such as large corporations, private businesses, law firms, hospitals and medical interest companies, museums, colleges, associations, and the government. These librarians are called corporate librarians, but are sometimes referred to as *special librarians, information specialists*, or *research librarians*.

Corporate librarians gather information of interest to their particular company. This material includes reference books, articles, reports, conferences, films and videos, and many other resources. This data is then organized, cataloged, and indexed into a working database that is accessible to the employees of the company.

Corporate librarians are available to help staff with a project or presentation by conducting research, verifying facts, or locating certain photos or film. At times, they may be asked to write reports, compile data, or do a background search on a particular topic. Much of their work is connected to the Internet; so corporate librarians are experts in computers and technology. They may also plan and implement training sessions for employees on the use of a new server or database. Corporate librarians must also keep current with trends and developments concerning their specific industries. Company time, energy, and resources are saved due to the work of corporate librarians.

The daily work of a corporate librarian is dependent on his or her place of employment. For example, a research librarian for a television network may be asked to provide background research or locate past film footage for a feature documentary. A pharmaceutical company may rely on an information specialist to compile data to help in the launch of a new drug. Government agencies or private organizations may rely on a special librarian to cull and archive decades of work or reports and other documents.

Three of the most popular types of corporate librarians are *medical librarians, law librarians*, and *advertising librarians*.

Medical librarians gather, organize, and present information dealing with health care issues, technological advances, and the work of other health care companies. They conduct research or contribute to reports on various medical topics such as diseases, new procedures, or courses of treatment. They also maintain and cross reference a collection of medical books, journals, and association reports. Medical librarians are well versed with online computer databases such as MEDLINE. They are employed by pharmaceutical companies, medical associations, hospitals, medical schools, and large health care companies.

Law librarians gather, organize, and present information of interest to law firms. They assist lawyers with case research and background checks. At times, they may be asked to research and write reports independently. They also manage the firm's collection of law books, reports, manuals, and corporate documents. They may also plan and conduct training sessions for staff and clients. Librarians working for firms specializing in patent law may also keep track of patents and trademarks. They should also have knowledge of Web-based services such as Westlaw and Lexis.

Advertising librarians gather, organize, and present information of interest to the particular agency or their clients. They may research industry trends, consumer preferences, specific brands or products, or competing agencies. Much of their work may revolve around video archives. For example, librarians employed at Leo Burnett maintain the Great Commercials Library, a huge collection of award-winning commercials. They code and organize these clips into a database. Employees can search the database by product or theme, and study the clips before preparing a new commercial pitch.

REQUIREMENTS

High School

A college preparatory course load is needed for this career—take classes in history, English, and speech, as well as business classes such as marketing and finance. Since the United States is rapidly becoming a multicultural society, it would be beneficial to be fluent in more than one language. Hone your writing skills; they will be important in writing reports or preparing presentations.

Much of the information accessed by corporate librarians is Internet based, so it is imperative to be comfortable working with computers. Know how to navigate the Internet. Get a head start by taking computer classes and fine-tuning your research skills on the Web.

If you plan on working in a particular specialty, then it would be wise to take related classes. For example, if you'd like to work as a librarian at the American Medical Association, you should take classes in biology, chemistry, and anatomy and physiology.

Postsecondary Training

To work as a corporate librarian, you will need a master of library science (M.L.S.) or master of library information science (M.L.I.S.)

degree. Schools offering this degree can be found throughout the United States, but programs accredited by the American Library Association (ALA) carry the most weight with prospective employers. There are nearly 50 ALA-accredited programs available in the United States, each lasting from one to two years. Some programs offer independent and/or distance learning options.

Many specialized librarians also earn a bachelor's degree that is complementary to their field. For example, corporate librarians working for financial institutions may have an undergraduate degree in business administration or finance. Those employed by advertising agencies may have an undergraduate degree in advertising. Medical librarians may have an educational background in science or work experience in the health care industry.

Some large law firms expect their corporate librarians to have a law degree in addition to an M.L.S./M.L.I.S. In fact, according to the American Association of Law Libraries, 30 percent of all law librarians have a law degree. Some schools now offer a combined M.L.S. and jurist doctor program, lasting about four years.

Certification or Licensing

Currently, there are no certification programs designed for this specialty. However, the SLA does offer annual conferences, continuing education classes, and a career development series to keep corporate librarians abreast of new technology and advancements in processing information.

Other Requirements

Corporate librarians need strong communication and interpersonal skills since a large part of their job is interacting with people in search of information—often on a tight deadline. They should also have excellent organization skills and be highly proficient in computers, the Internet, and related technologies. Corporate librarians also need to have a strong background in their particular specialty. For example, an advertising librarian should have knowledge of the advertising industry and be familiar with industry companies, publications, lingo, and trends.

EXPLORING

The ALA and SLA Web sites offer a wealth of information on accredited programs, curriculum, and scholarships and grants. Library associations dealing with a particular industry, such as the American Association of Law Libraries or the Medical Library Association, can also provide career insight, job hotlines, salary surveys, and access to online discussion groups. You can also read books and magazines about the field, and you should ask your school counselor to arrange an information interview with a corporate librarian.

EMPLOYERS

Corporate librarians can find work in a variety of industries. A limitless supply of information is now available to companies thanks to the Internet, but it demands a trained professional to sort, assess, and organize this data. Employment possibilities are excellent throughout the United States, but if you desire to work for a Fortune 500 company be prepared to relocate to a metropolitan area, such as New York City, Chicago, or Los Angeles. Association or nonprofit work is more plentiful in Washington, D.C., or nearby Arlington, Virginia.

STARTING OUT

It's almost impossible to be hired as a corporate librarian without an M.L.S. or M.L.I.S. However, students enrolled in an accredited program may be able find an internship or part-time work as an assistant librarian. Having an undergraduate degree and solid work experience related to the interests of your potential employer is helpful. Contact your school's career services office for potential job leads; oftentimes companies rely on library schools for their recruitment needs. Don't forget to check the job boards section found at library association Web sites (such as the Special Libraries Association, http://www.sla.org/careers) or job listings in library-related publications.

ADVANCEMENT

While new M.L.S. graduates can land full-time positions, those without relevant work experience may have to start their careers as assistant librarians. A typical route of advancement would be to the position of director or manager of the library, overseeing a staff of less experienced librarians and nonprofessional workers such as clerical help. However, much depends on the size of the company and its library budget. It is not uncommon for smaller companies to have a library staff of one. Corporate librarians can also advance their career by transferring to larger companies with bigger libraries.

Some corporate librarians choose to become independent consultants in their area of specialty. Companies without the resources or constant need to have their own facility often turn to freelancers to manage special projects. A small communications firm may contract a consultant to research technology trends or identify sectors of industry. Associations may enlist outside help in organizing data for a newly designed Web site.

EARNINGS

Salaries for corporate librarians vary by type of employer, geographic region, and the experience of the librarian. The Special Libraries Association reports that the average salary for special librarians was $73,880. Salaries for all librarians ranged from less than $33,480 to more than $82,450 in 2009, according to the U.S. Department of Labor (DOL).

Corporate librarians who are employed full time are usually eligible for fringe benefits such as paid vacation time, holiday pay, sick days, health insurance, and the opportunity to participate in retirement savings plans.

WORK ENVIRONMENT

Corporate librarians typically work in an office setting. Unlike reference librarians, those employed at corporations have little routine to their day. Tasks will vary depending on the project and deadline at hand. An advertising librarian, for example, may do research on consumer preferences one day and switch to archiving photos the next.

At times, the work may be demanding, especially when multiple projects are assigned. Corporate librarians also need to keep up with new sources of information and constantly changing technology. They can suffer from eyestrain due to the large amount of time they spend working in front of the computer monitor or reading references in print.

Most corporate librarians maintain the same hours as other company employees who work outside of the library department. A normal workweek is 35 to 40 hours, though some overtime work may be necessary to meet an important deadline. Because corporate librarians do much of their work independently, flextime or telecommuting is common in this field. Some corporate librarians choose to work on a part-time basis.

OUTLOOK

The DOL predicts that employment for all librarians will grow about as fast as the average through 2018. Opportunities for librarians who work in nontraditional settings (such as corporations) will be even stronger.

Since corporate librarians work in many different sectors of the economy, job prospects will vary based on the overall economic health of the industry in which the corporate librarian is employed. Currently, the strongest industries for corporate librarians are pharmaceuticals and law and medical organizations.

FOR MORE INFORMATION

For information on careers in law librarianship, contact
American Association of Law Libraries
105 West Adams Street, Suite 3300
Chicago, IL 60603-6225
Tel: 312-939-4764
http://www.aallnet.org

For a list of accredited schools and information on careers, scholarships and grants, and membership, contact
American Library Association
50 East Huron Street
Chicago, IL 60611-2729
Tel: 800-545-2433
http://www.ala.org

For more on information science careers, contact
American Society for Information Science and Technology
1320 Fenwick Lane, Suite 510
Silver Spring, MD 20910-3560
Tel: 301-495-0900
E-mail: asis@asis.org
http://www.asis.org

For information on careers in medical librarianship, contact
Medical Library Association
65 East Wacker Place, Suite 1900
Chicago, IL 60601-7246
Tel: 312-419-9094
E-mail: info@mlahq.org
http://www.mlanet.org

For information on careers in music librarianship, contact
Music Library Association
8551 Research Way, Suite 180
Middleton, WI 53562-3567
Tel: 608-836-5825
E-mail: mla@areditions.com
http://www.musiclibraryassoc.org

For information on working in a specialized library, contact
Special Libraries Association
331 South Patrick Street
Alexandria, VA 22314-3501
Tel: 703-647-4900
http://www.sla.org

For information on the field of competitive intelligence, contact
Strategic and Competitive Intelligence Professionals
1700 Diagonal Road, Suite 600
Alexandria, VA 22314-2863
Tel: 703-739-0696
E-mail: info@scip.org
http://www.scip.org

To receive information on librarianship in Canada, contact
Canadian Library Association
1150 Morrison Drive, Suite 400
Ottawa, ON K2H 8S9 Canada
Tel: 613-232-9625
E-mail: info@cla.ca
http://www.cla.ca

Database Specialists

QUICK FACTS

School Subjects
Computer science
Mathematics

Personal Skills
Mechanical/manipulative
Technical/scientific

Work Environment
Primarily indoors
Primarily one location

Minimum Education Level
Bachelor's degree

Salary Range
$40,780 to $71,550 to
$114,200+

Certification or Licensing
Voluntary

Outlook
Much faster than the average

DOT
039

GOE
02.06.01

NOC
2172

O*NET-SOC
15-1061.00

OVERVIEW

Database specialists design, install, update, modify, maintain, and repair computer database systems to meet the needs of their employers. To do this work they need strong math skills, the ability to work with many variables at once, and a solid understanding of the organization's objectives. They consult with other management officials to discuss computer equipment purchases, determine requirements for various computer programs, and allocate access to the computer system to users. They might also direct training of personnel who use company databases regularly. Database specialists may also be called *database designers, database analysts, database managers, database administrators*, or *information architects* in some businesses; while at other businesses, the designations database designer, analyst, manager, and administrator or information architect represent separate jobs but all fall under the umbrella category of database specialist. There are approximately 120,400 database administrators working in all industries in the United States.

HISTORY

During the 1950s, computers were big—they easily filled entire warehouses—and they were not considered practical for anything other than large government and research projects. However, by 1954, the introduction of semiconductors made computers smaller and more accessible to businesses. Within 30 years, computers had influenced nearly every aspect of life, such as work, entertainment, and even shopping. Today, computers are everywhere. Technology has continued to make computers smaller, more productive, and more efficient.

Technological advances have made database computing a subfield of tremendous growth and potential. Libraries, businesses, and other organizations use databases to replace existing paper-based procedures but also create new uses for them every day. For example, catalog companies use databases to organize inventory and sales systems, which before they did by hand. These same companies are pushing technology further by investigating ways to use databases to customize promotional materials. Instead of sending the same catalog out to everyone, some companies are looking to send each customer a special edition filled with items he or she would be sure to like, based on past purchases and a personal profile.

Database specialists are crucial participants in database development. In fact, many companies that took an inexpensive route to database computing by constructing them haphazardly are now sorry they did not initially hire a specialist. Designing the database structure is important because it translates difficult, abstract relationships into concrete, logical structures. If the work is done well to begin with, the database will be better suited to handle changes in the future.

Most commercial computer systems make use of some kind of database. As computer speed and memory capacity continue to increase, databases will become increasingly complex and able to handle a variety of new uses. Therefore, the individuals and businesses that specialize in inputting, organizing, and making available various types of information stand at the forefront of an ever-growing field.

THE JOB

So just what is a database and how is it used? It may be easiest to think of a database as being the computer version of the old-fashioned file cabinet that is filled with folders containing important information. The database is the important information, and the database specialist is the person who designs or adjusts programs for the way the information is stored, how separate pieces of information relate and affect one another, and how the overall system should be organized. For example, a specialist may set up a library's user database to have a separate "record" for each user, in the same way that the library may have had a separate file folder in its file cabinet for each user. In the library's user database, each transaction will have a separate record. Each record contains many "fields" where specific pieces of information are entered. Examples of fields for the user database include user number, user name, address, city, state, zip code, phone, and e-mail. With information organized in separate fields, the library can easily sort customer records, just like filing file folders in a file cabinet. In this way, the library can track overdue books, obtain contact information if a book is overdue, etc. Libraries also use databases to input and track inventory, monitor loans to other libraries, manage budgets, and facilitate a variety of other tasks.

Database specialists are responsible for the flow of computer information within an organization. They make major decisions concerning computer purchases, system designs, and personnel training. Their duties combine general management ability with a detailed knowledge of computer programming and systems analysis.

The specific responsibilities of a database specialist are determined by the size and type of employer. For example, a database specialist for a library system may develop a system for tracking late fees owed by customers, while a database specialist for a large corporation may develop a system for keeping track of important documents and other resources. To do this work accurately, database specialists need a thorough knowledge and understanding of the company's computer operations.

There are three main areas of the database specialist's work: planning what type of computer system an organization needs; implementing and managing the system; and supervising computer room personnel.

To adequately plan a computer system, database specialists must have extensive knowledge of the latest computer technology and the specific needs of their organization. They meet with high-ranking managers, such as the library director or library commissioner (who oversees libraries in an entire city or region), and together they decide how to apply the available technology to the organization's needs. Decisions include what type of hardware and software to order and how the data should be stored. Database specialists must be aware of the cost of the proposed computer system as well as the budget within which the organization is operating. Long-term planning is also important. Specialists must ensure that the computer system can process not only the existing level of computer information that will be made available to users, but also the anticipated load and type of information the organization could offer in the future.

Implementing and managing a computer system entails a variety of technical and administrative tasks. Depending on the organization's needs, the specialist may modify a system already in place, develop a whole new system, or tailor a commercial system to meet these needs. To do this type of work the database specialist must be familiar with accounting principles and mathematical formulas. Scheduling access to the computer system is also a key responsibility. Sometimes, database specialists work with representatives from all the departments to create a schedule. The specialist prioritizes needs and monitors usage so that each department can do its work. All computer usage must be documented and stored for future reference.

Safeguarding the computer operations is another important responsibility of database specialists. They must make plans in case a computer system fails or malfunctions so that the information stored in the computer is not lost. A duplication of computer files may be a part of this emergency planning. A backup system must also be employed so that the organization can continue to process information. Database specialists must also safeguard a system so that only authorized personnel have access to certain information. Computerized information may be of vital importance to an organization, and database specialists ensure that it does not fall into the wrong hands.

Database specialists may also supervise the work of personnel in the computer department. They may need to train new computer personnel hires to use the organization's database, and they may also need to train all computer personnel when an existing database is modified. At some organizations, specialists are also required to train all employees in the use of an upgraded or a new system. Therefore, specialists need the ability to translate technical concepts into everyday language.

Database specialists may be known by a number of different titles and have a variety of responsibilities, depending on the size and the needs of the organizations that employ them. According to an article in *Computerworld*, the title database designer or information architect indicates someone who works on database programming. These workers usually have a math or engineering background. The title database administrator indicates someone who primarily focuses on the performance of the database, making sure everything is running smoothly. They may also do routine jobs, such as adding new users to the system. The title database analyst indicates someone who primarily focuses on the business, its goals, products, and customers (or the library's goals, resources, and users). They work on improving the database so that the organization can meet its goals. In large businesses or organizations the many duties of the database specialist may be strictly divided among a number of specialists based on their titles. In smaller organizations there may be only one database specialist, designer, manager, administrator, or analyst who is responsible for carrying out all the tasks mentioned above.

No matter what their title is, however, all database specialists work with an operation that processes millions of bits of information at a huge cost. This work demands accuracy and efficiency in decision-making and problem-solving abilities.

REQUIREMENTS

High School

While you are in high school, take as many math, science, and computer classes as you can. These courses will provide you with the basics as well as begin to develop your logical thinking skills. Take electronics or other technical courses that will teach you about schematic drawing, working with electricity, and, again, develop logical thinking. You will also benefit from taking accounting courses and English classes. To be able to do this work well, you will need strong communication skills, both written and verbal.

Postsecondary Training

A bachelor's degree in computer science, computer information systems, database management or administration, or another computer-related discipline is recommended as the minimum requirement for those wishing to work as database specialists. Some exceptions have been made for people without a degree but who have extensive experience in database administration. Taking this route to become a database specialist, however, is becoming increasingly rare. Most employers will expect you to have at least a four-year degree. A bachelor's degree program usually includes courses in data processing, systems analysis methods, more detailed software and hardware concepts, management principles, and information systems planning. To advance in the field, you will probably need to complete further education. Many businesses today, especially larger companies, prefer database managers to have a master's degree in computer science or business administration. If you plan to work in library science, you should consider minoring in library science or at least taking some classes in the field to help you learn more about the particular technical challenges of creating and managing library databases. Some employers offer to help with or pay for their employees' advanced education, so you may want to consider this possibility when looking for an entry-level job.

Certification or Licensing

Some database specialists become certified for jobs in the computer field by passing an examination given by the Institute for Certification of Computing Professionals. DAMA, Data Management

International offers the certified data management professional designation to database professionals who meet education and experience requirements and pass an examination. For further information, contact the appropriate organizations listed at the end of this article. Specialists who want to keep their skills current may take training programs offered by database developers, such as Oracle. These programs may also lead to certifications.

Other Requirements
Database specialists are strong logical and analytical thinkers. They excel at analyzing massive amounts of information and organizing it into a coherent structure composed of complicated relationships. They are also good at weighing the importance of each element of a system and deciding which ones can be omitted without diminishing the quality of the final project.

Specialists also need strong communication skills. This work requires contact with employees from a wide variety of jobs. Specialists must be able to ask clear, concise, and technical questions of people who are not necessarily familiar with how a database works.

As is true for all computer professionals, specialists should be motivated to keep up with technological advances and able to learn new things quickly. Those who are interested in working almost exclusively in one industry (for example, health care) should be willing to gain as much knowledge as possible about that specific field in addition to their computer training. With an understanding of both fields of knowledge, individuals are more easily able to apply computer technology to the specific needs of the company.

EXPLORING

There are a number of ways to explore your interest in this field while you are still in high school. "Start by reading books on the subject," says Scott Sciaretta, an internal database consultant for ChoicePoint in Atlanta, Georgia. "There are hundreds of them at most bookstores."

You can also join your high school's computer club to work on computer projects and meet others interested in the field. Learn everything you can about computers by working with them regularly. Online sources can be particularly good for keeping up-to-date with new developments and learning from people who are actively involved in this work. Learn to use a commercial database program, either by teaching yourself or taking a class in it. The Association for Computing Machinery has a Special Interest Group on Management of Data (SIGMOD). The Resources page of SIGMOD's Web site (http://www.sigmod.org) provides an index of public domain database software that you may want to check out.

You may also want to ask your school counselor or a computer teacher to arrange for a database specialist to speak to your class at school or to arrange for a field trip to a company to see database specialists at work. Another option is to ask your school administrators about databases used by the school and try to interview any database specialists working in or for the school system. Similar attempts could be made with charities in your area that make use of computer databases for membership and client records as well as mailing lists.

Look for direct-experience opportunities, such as part-time work, summer internships, and even summer camps that specialize in computers. "Try to get a job as an intern in a database shop and learn by watching, mentoring, and grunt work," Sciaretta recommends. If you can't find such a position, you can still put your skills to work by offering to set up small databases, such as address books, recipe databases, or DVD libraries for friends or family members.

EMPLOYERS

Approximately 120,400 database administrators are employed in all industries in the United States today. Any business or organization that uses databases as a part of its operations hires database professionals. Database specialists work for libraries, museums, investment companies, telecommunications firms, banks, insurance companies, publishing houses, hospitals, school systems, universities, and a host of other large and midsize businesses and nonprofit organizations. There are also many opportunities with federal, state, and city governments.

STARTING OUT

Most graduating college students work closely with their school's career services office to obtain information about job openings and interviews. Local and national employers often recruit college graduates on campus, making it much easier for students to talk with many diverse companies. Another good source of information is through summer internships, which are completed typically between junior and senior year. Many major companies in the computer field, such as Intel (http://www.intel.com/about/corporateresponsibility/education/index.htm) and Oracle (http://www.oracle.com/us/corporate/careers/index.html), have established undergraduate intern programs. This experience is valuable for two reasons. First, it gives students hands-on exposure to computer-related jobs. Second, it allows students to network with working computer professionals who may help them find full-time work after graduation. Interested individuals might also scan the classified ads or work with temporary agencies or headhunters to find entry-level and mid-level positions. Professional organizations, such as SIGMOD, and professional publications are other sources of information about job openings.

ADVANCEMENT

The job of database specialist is in itself a high-level position. Advancement will depend to some extent on the size of the business the specialist works for, with larger companies offering more opportunities for growth at the mid-level and senior levels of management. Sciaretta explains his career path and advancement this way: "I got my first job in the field by internal promotion. Basically, I was doing some computer programming for my department on the side to automate a few of the menial tasks. My work got noticed, and I was given the job of running the company's computer department when the position opened. At my current level, the advancement opportunities are not easy. For me to advance I either need to expand my scope or work for a larger company, both of which are very feasible with hard work. However, salary advancements are easy and can be quite large. There are many opportunities for advancement from entry-level or junior positions."

Another factor influencing advancement is the interests of each individual. Generally, people fall into two categories: those who want to work on the business side and those who prefer to stay in a technical job. For individuals who want to get into the managerial side of the business, formal education in business administration is usually required, usually in the form of a master's degree in business administration. In upper-level management positions, specialists must work on cross-functional teams with professionals in finance, sales, personnel, purchasing, and operations. Superior database specialists at larger companies may also be promoted to executive positions.

Some database specialists prefer to stay on the technical side of the business. For them, the hands-on computer work is the best part of their job. Advancement for these workers will, again, involve further education in terms of learning about new database systems, gaining certification in a variety of database programs, or even moving into another technology area such as software design or networking.

As specialists acquire education and develop solid work experience, advancement will take the form of more responsibilities and higher wages. One way to achieve this is to move to a better paying, more challenging database position at a larger company. Some successful database specialists become high-paid consultants or start their own businesses. Teaching, whether as a consultant or at a university or community college, is another option for individuals with high levels of experience.

EARNINGS

A fairly wide range of salaries exists for database specialists. Earnings vary with the size, type, and location of the organization as well as a person's experience, education, and job responsibilities. According to the U.S. Department of Labor (DOL), median annual earnings for database administrators were $71,550 in 2009. The lowest paid 10 percent earned less than $40,780, while the highest paid 10 percent earned more than $114,200. Those who were employed by colleges and universities had mean annual earnings of $65,270.

Benefits for database professionals depend on the employer; however, they usually include such items as health insurance, retirement or 401(k) plans, and paid vacation days.

WORK ENVIRONMENT

Database specialists work in modern offices, usually located next to the computer room. If they work as consultants, they may travel to client sites as little as once or twice per project or as often as every week. Most duties are performed at a computer at the individual's desk. Travel is occasionally required for conferences and visits to affiliated database locations. Travel requirements vary with employer, client, and level of position held. Database specialists may need to attend numerous meetings, especially during the planning stages of a project. They work regular 40-hour weeks but may put in overtime as deadlines approach. During busy periods, the work can be quite stressful since accuracy is very important. Database specialists must therefore be able to work well under pressure and respond quickly to last-minute changes. Emergencies may also require specialists to work overtime or long hours without a break, sometimes through the night.

"I like what I do," Sciaretta says. "The hours are flexible. You get to work on and set up million-dollar systems. There also is a high degree of visibility from upper management. The downside is that I work lots of hours, including many weekends, and I have a never-ending list of work. The hardest part of the job is juggling the schedules and configurations for many projects at one time."

OUTLOOK

The use of computers and database systems in almost all business settings creates tremendous opportunities for well-qualified database personnel. As a result, employment for database specialists is expected to grow much faster than the average for all careers through 2018, according to the DOL.

Employment opportunities for database specialists should be best in large urban areas because of the multitudes of businesses and organizations located there that need employees to work with their databases. Since smaller communities are also rapidly developing significant job opportunities, skilled workers can pick from a wide range of jobs throughout the country. Those with the best education and the most experience in computer systems and personnel management will find the best job prospects.

FOR MORE INFORMATION

For information on library careers, contact
American Library Association
50 East Huron Street
Chicago, IL 60611-2729
Tel: 800-545-2433
http://www.ala.org

To learn more about information science careers, contact
American Society for Information Science and Technology
1320 Fenwick Lane, Suite 510
Silver Spring, MD 20910-3560
Tel: 301-495-0900
E-mail: asis@asis.org
http://www.asis.org

For information on education and awards programs, contact
Association for Educational Communications and Technology
PO Box 2447
Bloomington, IN 47402-2447
Tel: 877-677-2328
E-mail: aect@aect.org
http://www.aect.org

For information on career opportunities and chapters for college students, contact

Association of Information Technology Professionals
401 North Michigan Avenue, Suite 2400
Chicago, IL 60611-4267
Tel: 800-224-9371
http://www.aitp.org

Data Management International is an organization for professionals involved in business intelligence and data management. Visit its Web site to read articles related to these issues in Information Management *magazine.*

DAMA, Data Management International
19239 North Dale Mabry Highway, #132
Lutz, FL 33548
Tel: 813-778-5495
E-mail: info@dama.org
http://www.dama.org

For information about scholarships, student membership, and careers, contact

IEEE Computer Society
2001 L Street, NW, Suite 700
Washington, DC 20036-4910
Tel: 202-371-0101
E-mail: membership@computer.org
http://www.computer.org

For more information about certification, contact

Institute for Certification of Computing Professionals
2350 East Devon Avenue, Suite 281
Des Plaines, IL 60018-4602
Tel: 800-843-8227
E-mail: office2@iccp.org
http://www.iccp.org

For information on continuing education programs and publications, contact

Library & Information Technology Association
c/o American Library Association
50 East Huron Street
Chicago, IL 60611-2795
Tel: 800-545-2433, ext. 4270

E-mail: lita@ala.org
http://www.lita.org

To read articles from the quarterly Data Engineering Bulletin, *produced by the IEEE Technical Committee on Data Engineering, visit*
Data Engineering Bulletin
http://tab.computer.org/tcde

For more information on the Association for Computing Machinery's special interest group on management of data, visit
Special Interest Group on Management of Data
http://www.acm.org/sigmod

Film and Video Librarians

OVERVIEW

Librarians who oversee a collection of films and videos housed within a library, school, or business are called *film and video librarians*, or *media librarians*. They are in charge of researching, reviewing, purchasing, cataloging, and archiving the films and videos in all forms. The scope of the collection is dependent upon the type of institution or business in which they are employed.

Film and video librarians may also plan special viewing events or film discussion groups, or give class lectures. They take into account industry reviews and popular trends, as well as the input of the library director, teachers, students, and library patrons, when making new acquisitions. Many times they also maintain and provide instruction on the use of audiovisual equipment.

HISTORY

Although the career of film and video librarian has grown in popularity over the last several decades due to technological innovations and the growth of the motion picture, television, and educational media industries, this career actually began more than a century ago, according to the article "The History of Media Librarianship: A Chronology," by Amy Loucks-DiMatteo. In 1894, the Library of Congress housed the first paper or contact prints of motion pictures, and film librarians were needed to manage this collection. By approximately 1910, the Bell & Howell Film Company had assembled a film library of more than 1,200 silent and sound motion

Did You Know?

- Sixty-two percent of U.S. adults have library cards.
- The average American checks out seven books a year.
- Nearly 98 percent of public libraries provide Internet access to the public.
- Academic and public reference librarians answer 5.7 million reference questions a week.
- Students make 1.8 billion visits to school library centers during the academic year.

Sources: American Library Association, *Quotable Facts About America's Libraries: 2010*; 2010 Harris Survey

pictures. And by 1924, the American Library Association (ALA) recognized the growing importance of audiovisual libraries by creating a Visual Methods Committee to provide support to library professionals in this subfield.

The audiovisual library field grew in popularity over the next four decades. Major developments included the establishment of the first library audiovisual course at Peabody College in 1935; the publication of the book *Audiovisual School Library Service* (by Margaret Rufsvold), which offered instruction on how to establish an instructional materials center, in 1949; and the merging of many audiovisual libraries and traditional libraries into cohesive units in the 1950s and 1960s.

The introduction of home video in the 1970s created strong demand for librarians who specialized in audiovisual materials. Today, opportunities continue to be good for film and video librarians as a result of technological advancements and the increasing popularity of film and video as methods of entertainment and education.

THE JOB

Libraries are no longer limited to traditional collections of books and periodicals; they now include all forms of media, including music, film, and video. Those in charge of a special department or collection of film and videos are called film and video librarians, or media librarians. Their duties are similar to that of reference librarians, except their expertise is in film and video in all formats. Film and video librarians work in all types of libraries: public, governmental, corporate or special, and schools.

Film and video librarians are responsible for maintaining their library's collection of film and video. They catalog the items into the library's database according to their title, subject matter, or by actors/actresses and director. To prepare each film or video for circulation, each must be put in a protective covering or case, labeled with the library's name and address, and given a barcode and checkout card. Film and video librarians also archive and preserve existing material. They may also be responsible for the purchase and maintenance of audiovisual equipment.

It is the film and video librarian's responsibility to ensure that the collection meets the specific interests of the institution. For example, medical libraries would be interested in health care issues; the library of a women's studies department would be interested in biographies, history, and events regarding women, women's rights, and other related issues. Film and video librarians at public institutions have the harder task of building a collection that appeals to different tastes or needs. They have a working knowledge of many different subject areas, including biographies of famous people, historical events, health, theater and the arts, popular culture, anime, and children's interests. This knowledge is important because they have to acquire items covering a plethora of topics and genres.

Librarians rely on reference guides, reviews, and recommendations from distributors when making important decisions on new acquisitions. They also take into account their department's budget, the school's curriculum, the needs of the educators, and patrons' requests. They must negotiate with distributors regarding pricing and public performance rights.

Film and video librarians may also plan special media events revolving around a film presentation or video night at their facility. In this instance, they would be responsible for scheduling the event, deciding on a theme, and marketing it to the public. At times, they may be asked by the school's faculty to help search for films to accompany a particular lesson plan or assignment. Librarians employed by government agencies may help acquire videos for special educational or training programs, such as a "Say No to Drugs" campaign.

Film and video librarians also have managerial duties. They hire, train, schedule, and supervise department staff. Along with the library director, or advisory board, they review the needs, policies, and direction of the department. They write reviews on new materials, compile bibliographies, and, at times, give a lecture on a particular film or video. They also help students or library patrons find information, answer questions, or give instruction on the proper use of audiovisual equipment. Film and video librarians rely on conferences, continuing education classes, and discussions with their peers to keep abreast of new technology or industry changes.

REQUIREMENTS

High School
Take classes in English, history, science, foreign languages, art, computer science, and mathematics to prepare for this career. Classes that require you to write numerous research papers will give you good experience in writing and utilizing different library resources. Film and video librarians will often give class lectures or hold discussion groups. If you dread speaking in front of a small group, consider taking a speech class or join the debate team to hone your verbal communication skills.

You should also take film classes or perhaps join a photography club. Such activities will give you familiarity with films outside of the mainstream and experience with different equipment.

Postsecondary Training
The direction you take in college depends largely on your place of employment. Many librarians working in a school setting hold an education degree with a specialization in media or information studies. Most, if not all, librarians working in college, corporate, or public libraries have a master's degree in library science (M.L.S.) or a master's degree in information systems (M.I.S.). It is important to have earned an M.L.S. or M.I.S. from a program that is accredited by the ALA. Most programs last from one to two years, with some schools offering off-site study opportunities. Many film and video librarians have a bachelor's degree in liberal arts and/or extensive experience in film.

Certification or Licensing
Certification and licensing requirements vary by state, county, and local government. Contact the school board in the area in which you plan to work for more information. If you work in a public elementary or secondary school, you will often be required to earn teacher's certification and a master's degree in education in addition to preparation as a librarian.

Other Requirements

Film and video librarians must, first and foremost, have a love of film and video, and be willing to continue to learn about new technology throughout their careers. They must also have strong organizational skills, an attentiveness to detail, and the ability to interact well with coworkers and library patrons.

EXPLORING

A part-time job at a local library or your school's media center is a great way to explore this career. As a student you will probably be assigned small clerical tasks such as staffing the circulation desk, or straightening the stacks, but with some experience you may be assigned duties with more responsibilities. You might be able to eventually work as a media center aide, who sets up and maintains audiovisual equipment.

What better way to nurture your love of movies than by working at your local video store? Not only will you have access to the newest releases, you'll gain familiarity with films in a variety of subject areas.

You may want to participate in online discussion groups to get a feel for the industry. The ALA sponsors the Video Round Table (http://www.ala.org/ala/mgrps/rts/vrt/aboutvrt/vrtwelcome.cfm), an organization that addresses the interests of those working with video collections, programs, and services in libraries. This service is available to all ALA members.

EMPLOYERS

Although film and video librarians can find work in public or school libraries, the demand for this specialty is greatest in special libraries or those found in larger academic institutions. Reference librarians who work in small neighborhood libraries, or in media centers hosted within a school, may have film and video duties incorporated into their job responsibilities. Large metropolitan libraries often will have a separate film department with multiple staff. Universities, associations, or the government will also have an extensive film collection to warrant employing a film and video librarian on a full- or part-time basis.

STARTING OUT

There are many ways to enter this field. Some teachers decide to become librarians after having a fulfilling career in education. Reference librarians with a strong interest in films may choose to specialize in film and video acquisitions. Employment as an assistant film and video librarian is a common starting point and a great way to learn about the job and gain work experience.

Visit association Web sites to investigate the educational and certification requirements of librarians, as they vary from state to state. The ALA offers a wealth of information on this subject, including a list of employment opportunities nationwide, available awards, as well as grant and scholarship information.

ADVANCEMENT

There are many advancement opportunities available to film and video librarians. Librarians who work in smaller facilities may transfer to larger libraries where opportunities for job promotions and advancement are greater. It is also possible to move from one type of library to another. A librarian at a large public library may be responsible for a vast collection of biographies, documentaries, and instructional videos covering many different topics. A film and video librarian working for a corporation or nonprofit would only collect items dealing with that organization's interests or goals.

With sufficient work experience and education, those interested in administration may work as head of a film and video department, or even as a library director.

EARNINGS

Salaries for film and video librarians depend on such factors as the location, size, and type of library, the amount of experience the librarian has, and the responsibilities of the position. According to the U.S. Department of Labor (DOL), librarians had median annual earnings of $53,710 in 2009. Ten percent earned less than $33,480, and 10 percent earned $82,450 or more. Librarians working in colleges and universities earned $59,530 in 2009, and those in elementary and secondary schools earned $57,950. Librarians employed in local government earned $49,920 in 2009. In the federal government, the average salary for all librarians was $79,550.

Most film and video librarians receive a standard benefits package that includes paid vacation time, holiday pay, compensated sick leave, various insurance plans, and retirement savings programs.

WORK ENVIRONMENT

Film and video librarians employed at schools or public institutions have busy, often varied days. They may be researching possible new additions to the current collection one day, and teaching library staff members how to search for titles using a new online catalog the next. Disruptions are common, as patrons and staff will often turn to the film and video librarian with questions regarding a new documentary, or where to find an old black-and-white classic. Librarians working at a small library may be responsible for all duties in the film and video department, from reviewing and purchasing, to cataloging and maintenance. Those employed at a larger institution may have more administrative duties such as hiring, training, and supervising departmental staff, as well as setting work schedules.

Film and video librarians working for a special library do not usually have much interaction with the public. Much of their work—such as reviewing new acquisitions, reading trade publications and catalogs, and corresponding with distributors—is done independently.

Film and video librarians usually work a typical 40-hour week, Monday through Friday, with some weekend or evening hours as required. Some film and video librarians work part time. Those employed in an academic setting follow the school's schedule of summer and holiday breaks. Librarians often suffer from eyestrain due to long hours in front of the computer or reading print materials. Stress is another complication of this job. Film and video librarians often have to deal with multiple projects and deadlines.

OUTLOOK

The DOL predicts that employment for librarians will grow about as fast as the average for all careers through 2018. Opportunities should also be good for film and video librarians as more and more films and videos are released to educate and entertain the public. As with most careers, film and video librarians with advanced degrees and knowledge of the latest technology will have the best employment prospects.

FOR MORE INFORMATION

For a list of accredited schools and information on careers, scholarships and grants, and membership, contact
American Library Association
50 East Huron Street
Chicago, IL 60611-2729
Tel: 800-545-2433
http://www.ala.org

To learn more about information science careers, contact
American Society for Information Science and Technology
1320 Fenwick Lane, Suite 510
Silver Spring, MD 20910-3560
Tel: 301-495-0900
E-mail: asis@asis.org
http://www.asis.org

The association is a membership organization for media technology centers.
National Association of Media and Technology Centers
PO Box 9844
Cedar Rapids, IA 52409-9844
Tel: 319-654-0608
http://www.namtc.org

For information on working in a specialized library, contact
Special Libraries Association
331 South Patrick Street
Alexandria, VA 22314-3501
Tel: 703-647-4900
http://www.sla.org

For information on librarianship in Canada, contact
Canadian Library Association
1150 Morrison Drive, Suite 400
Ottawa, ON K2H 8S9 Canada
Tel: 613-232-9625
E-mail: info@cla.ca
http://www.cla.ca

Information Brokers

QUICK FACTS

School Subjects
Computer science
English
Journalism

Personal Skills
Communication/ideas
Technical/scientific

Work Environment
Primarily indoors
Primarily one location

Minimum Education Level
Bachelor's degree

Salary Range
$15,000 to $73,880 to
$200,000+

Certification or Licensing
None available

Outlook
Faster than the average

DOT
N/A

GOE
N/A

NOC
N/A

O*NET-SOC
N/A

OVERVIEW

Information brokers, sometimes called *online researchers, info-entrepreneurs,* or *independent information professionals*, compile information from online databases and services. They work for clients in a number of different professions, researching marketing surveys, newspaper articles, business and government statistics, abstracts, and other sources of information. They prepare reports and presentations based on their research. Information brokers have home-based operations, or they work full time for libraries, law offices, government agencies, and corporations.

HISTORY

Strange as it may seem, some of the earliest examples of information brokers are the keepers of a library established by Ptolemy I in Egypt in the 3rd century B.C. These librarians helped to build the first great library by copying and revising classical Greek texts. The monks of Europe also performed some of the modern-day researcher's tasks by building libraries and printing books. Despite their great efforts, libraries weren't used extensively until the 18th century, when literacy increased among the general population. In 1803, the first public library in the United States opened in Connecticut.

In the late 1800s and early 1900s, many different kinds of library associations evolved, reflecting the number of special libraries already established (such as medical and law libraries). With all the developments of the 20th century, these library associations helped to promote special systems and tools for locating information. These systems eventually developed into the online databases and Internet search engines used today.

THE JOB

An interest in the Internet and computer skills are important for success as an independent information broker, but this specialist needs to understand much more than just search engines. Information brokers need to master Dialog, Lexis/Nexis, and other information databases. They also have to compile information by using fax machines, photocopiers, and telephones, as well as by conducting personal interviews. If you think this sounds like the work of a private eye, you are not far off; as a matter of fact, some information brokers have worked as private investigators.

A majority of research projects, however, are marketing based. Suppose a company wants to embark on a new, risky venture—maybe a fruit distribution company wants to make figs as popular as apples and oranges. First, the company's leaders might want to know some basic information about fig consumption. How many people have even eaten a fig? What articles about figs have been published in national magazines? What have been recent annual sales of figs, Fig Newtons, and other fig-based treats? What popular recipes include figs? The company hires consultants, marketing experts, and researchers to gather all this information.

Each researcher has his or her own approach to accomplishing tasks, but every researcher must first get to know the subject. A researcher who specializes in retail and distribution might already be familiar with the trade associations, publications, and other sources of industry information. Another researcher might have to learn as much as possible, as quickly as possible, about the lingo and organizations involved with the fruit distribution industry. This includes using the Internet's basic search engines to get a sense of what kind of information is available. The researcher then uses a database service, such as the Dialog system, which makes available billions of pages of text and images, including complete newspaper and magazine articles, wire service stories, and company profiles. Because database services often charge the user for the time spent searching or documents viewed, online researchers must know all the various tips and commands for efficient searching. Once the search is complete and they've downloaded the information needed, online researchers must prepare the information for the company. They may be expected to make a presentation to the company or write a complete report that includes pie graphs, charts, and other illustrations to accompany the text.

The legal profession hires information brokers to search cases, statutes, and other sources of law; update law library collections; and locate data to support cases, such as finding expert witnesses, or researching the history of the development of a defective product that caused personal injury. The health care industry needs information brokers to gather information on drugs, treatments, devices, illnesses, or clinical trials. An information broker who specializes in public records researches personal records (such as birth, death, marriage, adoption, and criminal records), corporations, and property ownership. Other industries that rely on information brokers include banking and finance, government and public policy, and science and technology.

"This isn't the kind of profession you can do right out of high school or college," says Mary Ellen Bates, an independent information professional based in Niwot, Colorado. "It requires expertise in searching the professional online services. You can't learn them on your own time; you have to have real-world experience as an online researcher. Many of the most successful information brokers are former librarians." Her success in the business has led her to serve as past president of the Association of Independent Information Professionals, to write and publish articles about the business, and to serve as a consultant to libraries and other organizations. Some of her projects have included research on the market for independent living facilities for senior citizens and the impact of large grocery chains on independent grocery stores. She's also been asked to find out what rental car companies do with cars after they're past their prime. "Keep in mind that you need a lot more than Internet research skills," Bates says. "You need the ability to run your business from the top to bottom. That means accounting, marketing, collections, strategic planning, and personnel management."

The expense of the commercial database services has affected the career of another online researcher, Sue Carver of Richland, Washington. Changes in Dialog's usage rates have forced her to seek out other ways to use her library skills. In addition to such services as market research and document delivery, Carver's Web page promotes a book-finding service, helping people to locate collectible and out-of-print books. "I have found this a fun, if not highly lucrative, activity which puts me in contact with a wide variety of people," she says. "This is a case where the Internet opens the door to other possibilities. Much of this business is repackaging information in a form people want to buy. This is limited only by your imagination." But she also emphasizes that the job of online researcher requires highly specialized skills in information retrieval. "Nonlibrarians often do not appreciate the vast array of reference material that existed before the Internet," she says, "nor how much librarians have contributed to the information age." Carver holds a master's degree in library science and has worked as a reference librarian, which involved her with searches on patents, molecular biology, and other technical subjects. She has also worked as an indexer on a nuclear engineering project and helped plan a search and retrieval system on a separate nuclear project.

REQUIREMENTS

High School

Take computer classes that teach word processing and data processing programs, presentation programs, and how to use Internet search engines. Any class offered by your high school or public library on information retrieval will familiarize you with database searches and such services as Dialog, Lexis/Nexis, and Dow Jones. English and composition courses will teach you to organize information and write clearly. Speech and theater classes will help you develop the skills to give presentations in front of clients. Journalism classes and working on your high school newspaper will involve you directly in information retrieval and writing.

Postsecondary Training

It is recommended that you start with a good liberal arts program in a college or university, and then pursue a master's degree in either a subject specialty or in library and information science. Developing expertise in a particular subject will prepare you for a specialty in information brokering.

Many online researchers have master's degrees in library science. The American Library Association accredits library and information science programs and offers a number of scholarships. Courses in library programs deal with techniques of data collection and analysis, use of graphical presentation of sound and text, and networking and telecommunications. Internships are also available in some library science programs.

Continuing education courses are important for online researchers with advanced degrees. Because of the rapidly changing technology, researchers need to attend seminars and take courses through such organizations as the Special Libraries Association. Many online researchers take additional courses in their subject matter specialization. Bates attends meetings of the Strategic and Competitive Intelligence Professionals (http://www.scip.org), since a lot of her work is in the field of competitive intelligence.

Other Requirements

In addition to all the varied computer skills necessary to succeed as an information broker, you must have good communication skills. "You're marketing all the time," Bates says. "If you're not comfortable marketing yourself and speaking publicly, you'll never make it in this business." To keep your business running, you need persistence to pursue new clients and sources of information. You are your own boss, so you have to be self-motivated to meet deadlines. Good record-keeping skills will help you manage the financial details of the business and help you keep track of contacts.

Carver advises that you keep up on current events and pay close attention to detail. You should welcome the challenge of locating hard-to-find facts and articles. "I have a logical mind," Carver says, "and love puzzles and mysteries."

EXPLORING

If you've ever had to write an extensive research paper, then you've probably already had experience with online research. In college, many of your term papers will require that you become familiar with Lexis/Nexis and other library systems. The reference librarians of your school and public libraries should be happy to introduce you to the various library tools available. On the Internet, experiment with the search engines; each service has slightly different features and capabilities.

Visit Bates's Web site at http://www.batesinfo.com for extensive information about the business and to read articles she's written. She's also the co-author of a number of books including *Building and Running a Successful Research Business: A Guide for the Independent Information Professional*. 2d ed. (Medford, N.J.: Information Today, 2010), *Super Searchers Cover the World: The Online Secrets of International Business Researchers* (Medford, N.J.: Information Today, 2001), and *Researching Online for Dummies*, 2d edition (Foster City, Calif.: IDG Books Worldwide, 2000).

EMPLOYERS

A large number of information professionals are employed by colleges, universities, and corporations, and gain experience in full-time staff positions before starting their own businesses. Those who work for themselves contract with a number of different kinds of businesses and organizations. People seeking marketing information make the most use of the services of information professionals. Attorneys, consulting firms, public relations firms, government agencies, and private investigators also hire researchers. With the Internet, a researcher can work anywhere in the country, serving clients all around the world. However, living in a large city will allow an online researcher better access to more expansive public records when performing manual research.

STARTING OUT

People become researchers through a variety of different routes. They may go into business for themselves after gaining a lot of experience within an industry, such as in aviation or pharmaceuticals. Using their expertise, insider knowledge, and professional connections, they can serve as a consultant on issues affecting the business. Or they may become an independent researcher after working as a special librarian, having developed computer and search skills. The one thing most researchers have in common, however, is extensive experience in finding information and presenting it. Once they have the knowledge necessary to start their own information business, online researchers should take seminars offered by professional associations. Amelia Kassel, president and owner of MarketingBase (http://www.marketingbase.com), a successful information brokering company, offers a mentoring program via e-mail. As a mentor, she advises on such subjects as online databases, marketing strategies, and pricing.

Before leaving her full-time job, Bates spent a year preparing to start her own business. She says, "I didn't want to spend time doing start-up stuff that I could spend marketing or doing paying work." She saved business cards and established contacts. She saved $10,000 and set up a home-based office with a computer, desk, office supplies, fax, and additional phone lines.

ADVANCEMENT

The first few years of any business are difficult and require long hours of marketing, promotion, and building a clientele. Advancement will depend on the online researcher's ability to make connections and to broaden his or her client base. Some researchers start out specializing in a particular area, such as in telephone research or public record research, before venturing out into different areas. Once they're capable of handling projects from diverse sources, they can expand their business. They can also take on larger projects as they begin to meet other reliable researchers with whom they can join forces.

EARNINGS

Even if they have a great deal of research experience, self-employed information brokers' first few years in the business may be lean ones, and they should expect to make as little as $15,000. As with any small business, it takes a few years to develop contacts and establish a reputation for quality work. Independent information brokers usually charge between $45 and $100 an hour, depending on the project. Eventually, an online researcher should be able to make a salary equivalent to that of a full-time special librarian—according to a 2009 salary survey by the Special Libraries Association that puts the national median at $73,880. Some very experienced independent researchers with a number of years of self-employment may make well over $200,000.

The average information broker charges $75 an hour. This hourly rate is affected by factors such as geographic location and the broker's knowledge of the subject matter. Information brokers can make more money in cities like New York and Washington, D.C., where their services are in higher demand. Also, someone doing high-level patent research, which requires a great deal of expertise, can charge more than someone retrieving public records.

Information brokers who work full time for companies earn salaries comparable to other information technology (IT) professionals. Salaries for IT professionals can range from less than $40,000 for entry-level personnel to more than $114,000 for those with more than 10 years' experience. A full-time information broker who works for a large corporation primarily in the area of competitive intelligence can earn $100,000 or more annually.

Benefits for full-time workers include vacation and sick time, health, and sometimes dental, insurance, and pension or 401(k) plans. Self-employed information brokers must provide their own benefits.

WORK ENVIRONMENT

Most independent researchers work out of their own homes. This means they have a lot of control over their environment, but it also means they're always close to their workstations. As a result, online researchers may find themselves working longer hours than if they had an outside office and a set weekly schedule. "This is easily a 50- to 60-hour a week job," Bates says. Online researchers are their own bosses, but they may work as a member of a team with other researchers and consultants on some projects. They will also need to discuss the project with their clients both before and after they've begun their research.

Information brokers employed by companies work in an office environment. Although most of their work takes place at a computer, they may have to make trips to libraries, government offices, and other places that hold information that's not available online. Whether self-employed or not, information brokers spend some time in boardrooms and conference situations making presentations of their findings.

OUTLOOK

The Internet is making it easier for people and businesses to conduct their own online research; this is expected to help business for online researchers rather than hurt. Alex Kramer, past president of the Association of Independent Information Professionals, predicts that the more people recognize the vast amount of information available to them, the more they'll seek out the assistance of online researchers to efficiently compile that information. There will be continuing demand for information brokers in marketing, competitive intelligence, legal research, and science and technology.

Employment experts predict that with the growing reliance on computer technology, businesses will be willing to pay top dollar for employees and consultants who are flexible, mobile, and able to navigate the technology with ease.

FOR MORE INFORMATION

For a list of accredited schools and information on careers, scholarships and grants, and membership, contact
American Library Association
50 East Huron Street
Chicago, IL 60611-2729
Tel: 800-545-2433
http://www.ala.org

To learn more about information science careers, contact
American Society for Information Science and Technology
1320 Fenwick Lane, Suite 510
Silver Spring, MD 20910-3560
Tel: 301-495-0900
E-mail: asis@asis.org
http://www.asis.org

To learn more about the career of information broker, contact
Association of Independent Information Professionals
8550 United Plaza Boulevard, Suite 1001
Baton Rouge, LA 70809-2256
Tel: 225-408-4400
E-mail: office@aiip.org
http://www.aiip.org

For information on working in a specialized library, contact
Special Libraries Association
331 South Patrick Street
Alexandria, VA 22314-3501
Tel: 703-647-4900
http://www.sla.org

Law Librarians

OVERVIEW

Law librarians are professionally trained librarians who work in legal settings such as court systems, private law firms, government libraries, corporate law departments, and law schools. There are approximately 159,900 librarians employed in the United States; a small percentage are law librarians.

HISTORY

As long as there have been lawyers, barristers, solicitors and the like, there have undoubtedly been collections of legal materials large or small—the precursors to law libraries of today. In the United States, the Library of Congress was established in 1800, essentially as a collection of, although not limited to, law books and other materials to aid Congress. During the next few decades, the desire to have the law books and materials housed separately from the rest of the collection gained support. Finally, in 1832, Congress ordered that the law books of the Library of Congress be separated from its general collection, thus establishing the Law Library of Congress.

The Library of Congress was not the only entity to see the benefits of having its own private library specializing in the legal materials they needed to do their jobs; other government agencies, businesses, and law firms also maintained such collections, and law libraries have became more prevalent.

Today's law libraries house more than law books. Their holdings include legal periodicals and documents, and, in recent years, have

Library Facts

There are approximately 122,101 libraries in the United States. The American Library Association reports the following breakdown by type of library:

School libraries: 99,180
>   public schools: 81,920
>   private schools: 17,100
>   Bureau of Indian Affairs: 160

Public libraries (administrative units): 9,221
>   centrals: 9,040
>   branches: 7,629

Special libraries: 8,476

Academic libraries: 3,827
>   less than four-year: 1,434
>   four-year and above: 2,393

Government: 1,113

Armed forces libraries: 284

grown to incorporate such technological advances as digital reference material and online databases.

THE JOB

Law librarians are the professionals upon whom countless lawyers, judges, law students, and faculty depend on to quickly fulfill research requests and guide them through the seemingly endless and ever-growing maze of legal books, periodicals, documents, digital databases, and other resources. The responsibilities of law librarians vary across different work environments, but ultimately, service and organization are essential to most duties performed by law librarians.

In general, law firms and law departments of corporations hire law librarians to maintain their libraries. The duties of a law librarian in a law firm or corporate law department include deciding what materials to add and what materials to weed out as necessary and cataloging the contents of the firm's collections. They may

A law librarian at the Yale University School of Law poses in the school's library. *(Bob Child, AP Photo)*

be responsible for creating budgets and supervising other support staff. They also may help their patrons navigate the large amount of specialized information available, either by helping someone find the resource that they need, or researching a specific topic as requested.

In addition to the tasks already mentioned, *academic law librarians* who work in college or university law libraries may have a stronger focus on instruction than other law librarians. They may work closely with law school professors and teach law school students where to look for specific information and how to use research tools efficiently.

Government law librarians work in government law offices, courts, prisons, and government agencies. They manage law-related materials for lawyers, judges, and other government officials.

Some law librarians work for outside vendor companies, usually in sales or training. They use their experience and knowledge of how a law library functions to sell and/or train law library staff about products and services that may meet the information needs of law library staff and patrons.

REQUIREMENTS

High School

To become a law librarian, you will need to go to college and graduate school, so it is necessary to take college preparatory courses while in high school. Classes in civics, government, and history will give you a useful introduction to law. English and computer science classes will also help you prepare for learning the skills you will need as a librarian. Take advantage of any assignments or classes that will allow you to build useful library research skills, such as writing a paper for your English or history class.

Postsecondary Training

A liberal arts college education will give you a well-rounded educational background. Consider taking some computer classes, since computers are used frequently in the modern library. You should also consider taking classes that strengthen your writing and communication skills, and any classes that have a strong focus on research methodology. While many accredited library schools do not require any introductory courses in library science as an undergraduate, it is a good idea to check with the schools you are considering for any specific requirements they may have.

The vast majority of law librarians have a master's degree—generally a master of library science (M.L.S.) or master of library and information science (M.L.I.S.). In fact, most positions in this field require a M.L.S./M.L.I.S. The graduate school you choose should be accredited by the American Library Association (ALA), as some law libraries do not consider job applicants who attended a unaccredited school.

A typical library study graduate program will include courses in reference and research work, cataloging, computers, library organization, collection management, and administration; a program with a focus on information science will include courses in the computer sciences, mathematics, and systems analysis.

According to the American Association of Law Libraries (AALL), program material geared for those specifically interested in a career as a law librarian should include courses focusing on the legal system—its branches and procedures; the legal profession and related terminology; literature of the law, such as print and electronic resources; and ethical considerations when dealing with the law. Some law librarians earn a law degree (called a juris doctor, or J.D.) in addition to their M.L.S. The additional degree may be earned separately, or you may chose to earn both degrees simultaneously; there are several schools that offer joint J.D./M.L.S. degrees. Joint programs are longer than typical library science graduate programs, as most J.D./M.L.S. programs take four or more years to complete. Visit http://www.aallnet.org/committee/rllc/resources/lawlib-state.asp for a list of joint programs. The American Association of Law Libraries estimates that fewer than 20 percent of law librarian positions require both a library science degree and a law degree.

Certification or Licensing

No certification or licensing is available for law librarians. Librarians who earn a law degree must be admitted to the bar of that state before they can practice. They require that applicants graduate from an approved law school and that they pass a written examination in the state in which they intend to practice.

Other Requirements

A law librarian must have strong organizational skills and an analytical mind to manage the day-to-day operations of a typical law library. Because they have to deal with lawyers, students, and judges, many of whom may be stressed from working under deadlines and who may want materials quickly, law librarians need strong communication skills, tactfulness, and the ability to maintain a calm demeanor in high-pressure circumstances.

Some positions in federal government law libraries may require civil service eligibility; contact the Office of Personnel Management for more information. As mentioned earlier, some law librarian positions require a law degree in addition to an M.L.S./M.L.I.S.

EXPLORING

If you are interested in becoming a law librarian, read as many books and periodicals about law and librarianship as you can. Visit the Web sites of professional associations to learn more about career options, educational requirements, and issues affecting the field. The American Association of Law Libraries offers an excellent Web site, http://www.lawlibrarycareers.org, for aspiring law librarians. It also offers *Careers in Law Librarianship*, a useful publication that provides an overview of the field. It can be accessed by visiting http://www.aallnet.org/committee/rllc/tips/recruitment-brochure.pdf. Ask your teacher or counselor to help arrange an information interview with a law librarian.

EMPLOYERS

Only a small percentage of the 159,900 librarians employed in the United States specialize in law librarianship. Law librarians work in college and university law libraries, libraries of law firms, the law departments of business corporations or other organizations, libraries of nonprofit legal aid and other organizations, and for the government (in prisons and in state, county, and city legal departments or courts). Law librarians also work for vendors of legal information resources as sales or training staff or liaisons who work with law librarians.

STARTING OUT

There are many options to keep in mind when searching for a job as a law librarian. Newspapers and trade journals are good job sources, but keep in mind that local government law libraries and law firms might only advertise job openings locally, whereas national and international law firms and academic law libraries tend to advertise their job openings nationally. Other good resources include the American Association of Law Librarians Web site, which has an online career center (http://www.aallnet.org/careers) that lists law library positions available across the country. It also has links to local AALL chapter Web sites, which list local job openings. The Special Library Association and the American Library Association post job openings for law librarians on their Web sites. Other useful library-related job-search and career resource sites include LisJobs. com (http://lisjobs.com) and Library Job Postings on the Internet (http://www.libraryjobpostings.org).

Some law librarians start out as clerks while going to school for their advanced degrees, thus acquiring experience in the actual work setting while gaining their education.

ADVANCEMENT

Law librarians advance by moving into managerial positions or taking positions at larger firms or organizations. Some law librarians may become college professors.

EARNINGS

Factors affecting earnings in this field include the amount of experience the law librarian has, the responsibilities of his or her position, the size and type of law library in which he or she is employed, and geographic location. Law librarians employed in larger cities tend to make more than their counterparts in smaller metropolitan areas. In 2009, mean salaries for librarians working in legal services were $66,370 or more, according to the U.S. Bureau of Labor Statistics. Those employed by colleges or universities earned mean annual salaries of $59,430. Overall annual earnings for librarians ranged from less than $33,480 to $82,450 or more.

Most law librarians receive paid vacation time, holiday pay, sick days, health insurance, and the opportunity to participate in retirement savings plans. Law librarians who work in a college or university law library may receive tuition discounts or waivers for themselves and their family members.

WORK ENVIRONMENT

Most law librarians spend much of their workday indoors in a generally pleasant environment. They may spend a great deal of time sitting at their desk and using computers, so eyestrain and headaches from continuous computer use are possible. Even though much of the material they work with may be electronic, law librarians still have to deal with the printed word. That means regularly lifting and carrying periodicals and books, some of which can be heavy. Their work environment can also be stressful, as they may work with lawyers, judges, or students who are working under deadline pressure.

Librarians who have taken positions in sales or training will likely have more opportunities for travel as they visit libraries both nearby as well as those in other cities, states, or countries. They are also more likely to have more independence than a typical law librarian and may work from home when they are not at sales or training appointments.

OUTLOOK

The U.S. Department of Labor (DOL) predicts that employment of lawyers will grow about as fast as the average for all occupations through 2018. This steady growth for lawyers, and the increasing complexity and sheer volume of legal materials, suggests that opportunities for law librarians will continue to remain good in the next decade. Librarians who stay up-to-date with the latest technology and education in the field will have the best employment prospects. Overall employment of librarians, regardless of specialty, is expected to grow about as fast as the average for all careers through 2018, according to the DOL.

FOR MORE INFORMATION

For information on careers in law librarianship, contact
American Association of Law Libraries
105 West Adams Street, Suite 3300
Chicago, IL 60603-6225
Tel: 312-939-4764
http://www.aallnet.org

For a list of accredited schools and information on careers, scholarships and grants, and membership, contact
American Library Association
50 East Huron Street
Chicago, IL 60611-2729
Tel: 800-545-2433
http://www.ala.org

To learn more about information science careers, contact
American Society for Information Science and Technology
1320 Fenwick Lane, Suite 510
Silver Spring, MD 20910-3560
Tel: 301-495-0900
E-mail: asis@asis.org
http://www.asis.org

For information on working in a specialized library, contact
Special Libraries Association
331 South Patrick Street
Alexandria, VA 22314-3501
Tel: 703-647-4900
http://www.sla.org

Librarians

OVERVIEW

As prominent professionals in the information services field, *librarians* help others find information and select materials best suited to their needs. Librarians work in public, academic, and special libraries; school library media centers; corporations; and government agencies. They are key personnel wherever books, magazines, audiovisual materials, and a variety of other informational materials are cataloged and kept. Librarians help make access to these reference materials possible. Approximately 159,900 librarians are employed in positions throughout the country.

HISTORY

It may be hard to believe, but libraries have been around since 3000 B.C. Ancient Sumerian libraries contained clay tablets with cuneiform inscriptions (written with a stylus) baked onto them, and Egyptian libraries housed hieroglyphic accounts recorded on papyrus rolls. These libraries were available only to members of royalty, very wealthy families, or religious groups that devoted time and effort to transcription. The people who were charged with caring for collections within these libraries could be considered the world's first librarians.

Libraries continued to be available only to the elite until the Middle Ages, when many private institutions were destroyed by wars. The preservation of many ancient library materials can be attributed to orders of monks who diligently copied ancient Greek and Roman texts, as well as the Bible and other religious texts, and protected materials in their monasteries. The invention of the printing press in the 15th century allowed books to be made more quickly and disseminated more widely. Books went from palaces and churches to the homes of the common people.

In 1638, John Harvard left his private collection of books to the Massachusetts Bay Colony's new college, which was later named for him; this collection became the foundation for the first library in the United States. In the 18th century, Benjamin Franklin initiated the idea of a library from which books could be borrowed. From these beginnings, thousands of public, private, and special libraries have grown, as has the need for trained professionals to manage the collections. The idea of a lending library brought librarians into a more public arena; they were no longer just the keepers of knowledge, but also the professionals who made information available to everyone.

Although the education and certification processes have changed drastically, the field of librarianship has been around since the first clay tablet was stored in an ancient government building. Long before formal courses of study were developed for the training of librarians, church and government leaders appointed educated, organized individuals to collect informational materials and store them in a manner that would enable materials to be found when needed. In 1627, Gabriel Naude wrote *Advice on Establishing a Library*, a practical guide on how to establish a library that offered suggestions on organizing and using collections of informational materials.

Over the years the duties of librarians have evolved along with the development of different kinds of libraries and the development of new technologies. In recent years libraries have expanded services and now distribute films, MP3s and compact discs, digital video discs (DVDs), videos, braille books, and audio books. A wealth of information is available through multimedia CD-ROMs, computer database vendors, and the Internet. Librarians are charged with effectively and efficiently utilizing—and teaching the public how to utilize—the information available to them. From ancient Egyptians carefully storing papyrus rolls, to monks of the Middle Ages copying down books of the Bible, to special collections librarians studying materials cared for by their predecessors, librarianship is a profession that crosses the boundaries of time and space.

THE JOB

Librarians perform a number of tasks depending on their specialties. Some librarians may focus entirely on user services while others are concerned with technical or administrative services. Depending on the needs of their departments or institutions, librarians may perform a combination of these tasks, or take care of even more specific duties within their specialty. Some specific types of librarians in each category are noted in the following paragraphs, but this is not an exhaustive list. If one of these areas interests you, be sure to contact a library school for information about additional opportunities.

The librarian working in user services helps patrons find materials and use resources effectively. This type of librarian should be thoroughly acquainted with all materials in the library, from card and online catalogs to reference books. *Reference librarians* advise users and help them find information they are seeking in encyclopedias, almanacs, reference books, computerized information databases, or other sources. They also have access to special materials that may be filed in areas not open to the public or kept off-site.

Often librarians in user services may choose to work with a special age group. *Children's librarians* help children select books, teach them about the library, and conduct story hours. (For more information on this career, see the article "Children's Librarians.") *Young-adult librarians* perform similar services for junior and senior high school students. Instead of story hours, however, they plan programs of interest to young adults, such as creative writing workshops, film discussion groups, music concerts, or photography classes. *Adult services librarians* work with the adult population. They may help conduct education programs in community development, creative arts, public affairs, problems of the aging, and home and family.

Law librarians are professionally trained librarians who work in legal settings such as private law firms, government libraries, and law schools. (For more information, see the article "Law Librarians.")

Medical librarians, also known as *medical information specialists*, help manage health information. They are employed in libraries or information centers in hospitals and other medical facilities, public libraries, government agencies, research centers, colleges and universities, and pharmaceutical, publishing, biotechnology, and insurance companies. (For more information, see the article "Medical Librarians.")

Music librarians perform many of the same duties as traditional librarians, but specialize in managing materials related to music. They are employed at large research libraries; colleges, universities, and conservatories; public libraries; radio and television stations; and musical societies and foundations. They also work for professional bands or orchestras and music publishing companies. (For more information, see the article "Music Librarians.")

Library media specialists work with young people in school settings. They select materials useful to students in their class work, teach them to use the library media center effectively, help them with assignments, and work with teachers on research. Also known as *audiovisual librarians*, library media specialists (who must also be certified as teachers) select and maintain films, videotapes, slides, prints, records, cassettes, DVDs, compact discs, and other nonbook materials and supervise the purchase and maintenance of the equipment needed to use these materials. (For more information, see the article "Library Media Specialists.")

Community outreach librarians or *bookmobile librarians* bring library services to outlying areas or to special communities such as nursing homes or inner-city housing projects. These librarians bring resources to communities that do not have easy access to library services.

The technical tasks of the librarian may include ordering, cataloging, and classifying materials according to the Dewey Decimal, Library of Congress, or other system, and librarians involved with these technical services might not deal with the public at all. These librarians select and order all books, periodicals, audiovisual materials, and other items for the library; this entails evaluating newly published materials as well as seeking out older ones. Many libraries now have added compact discs, audio recordings, DVDs, films and videos, computer and video games, slides, maps, art pieces, and photographs to their loan services. The selection and purchase of these is also the responsibility of the librarian. The librarian, therefore, considerably influences the quality and extent of a library collection.

All new additions to the library must be cataloged by title, author, and subject in computerized catalog files. Labels, card pockets, and barcodes must be placed on the items, and they must then be properly shelved. Books and other materials must be kept in good condition and, when necessary, repaired or replaced. Librarians are also charged with purchasing, maintaining, and evaluating the circulation system. Considerable technical knowledge of computer systems may be necessary in deciding upon the extent and scope of the proper circulation for the library. The actual process of circulating books, such as stamping due dates, collecting fines, and tracking down overdue materials, however, is usually handled by nonprofessional library staff such as work-study students, part-time employees, technicians, or assistants.

Acquisitions librarians choose and buy books and other media for the library. They must read product catalogs and reviews of new materials as part of the acquisitions decision process. They do not work with the public, but deal with publishers and wholesalers of new books, booksellers of out-of-print books, and distributors of audiovisual materials. (For more information, see the article

"Acquisitions Librarians.") When the ordered materials arrive, *cataloging librarians* classify the items by subject matter, assign classification numbers, and prepare computer records to help users locate the materials. (For more information, see the article "Cataloging Librarians.") Since libraries have computerized the acquisitions and cataloging functions, it is now possible for the user to retrieve materials faster, using computer terminals instead of bulky card catalogs.

Bibliographers usually work in research libraries, compiling lists of books, periodicals, articles, and audiovisual materials on selected topics. They also recommend the purchase of new materials in their special fields. *Information scientists*, or *automated-systems librarians*, are specialists trained in computer sciences who plan and operate computer systems. More and more libraries today are tied into remote computer databases through their computer terminals, making it unnecessary for a library to house all the materials users may request. *Information architects* are information scientists who design systems for storing and retrieving information. They also develop procedures for collecting, organizing, interpreting, and classifying information.

Circulation librarians, with the help of clerical workers and stack attendants, manage the records of books and materials that are borrowed and returned and make sure that the materials are returned to the appropriate place in the library. *Conservation librarians* are charged with protecting and lengthening the life of the library collection. These librarians plan for the future, preparing for circumstances that might threaten the collections.

Administrative services librarians manage all areas of the library. They supervise library personnel and prepare budgets. They are also responsible for public relations and represent the library within its community as well as in such policy-making organizations as state or national library associations. Ultimately, administrators make sure that the library is constantly cultivating and expanding its resources to best serve the needs of its community.

The *library director* is at the head of a typical library organizational scheme. This individual sets library policies and plans and administers programs of library services, usually under the guidance of a governing body, such as a board of directors or board of trustees. Library directors have overall responsibility for the operation of a library system. (For more information, see the article "Library Directors.") Among their many duties, they coordinate the activities of the *chief librarians*, who supervise branch libraries or individual departments, such as the circulation, general reference, or music departments; periodical reading room; or readers' advisory service. In a large public library, a chief librarian supervises a staff

A bookmobile librarian provides some book suggestions for a patron.
(*Jenni Farrow*, The Daily Reflector/AP Photo)

of *assistant librarians* and *division heads* while administering and coordinating the functions of the library.

The *assistant librarians* often consult with (and report to) the chief librarian or library director regarding policy decisions for their area. They also train, schedule, and supervise *library technicians* and *library assistants*. Library technicians and assistants work in all areas of library services. They assist patrons in the library, on the telephone, and via e-mail, and they provide information on library services, facilities, and rules. They also catalog materials, prepare orders of materials and books, maintain files, work on checkouts, and perform many other varieties of jobs within specialized areas such as audiovisual or data processing. (For more information, see the articles "Library Technicians" and "Library Assistants.")

REQUIREMENTS

High School

If you are interested in becoming a librarian, be sure to take a full college preparatory course load. Focus on classes in history, English, speech, and foreign languages if you are going into user services. If you plan on working in a special library, take classes related to that specialty. For instance, if science is your interest, take courses such as anatomy, biology, chemistry, and physics. Learning how to use a computer and conduct basic research in a library is essential. Developing these skills will not only aid in your future library work, but will also help you in college and in any other career options you might pursue.

Postsecondary Training

Consider enrolling in a liberal arts college to get a broad educational background, since librarians should be familiar with numerous subject areas. While an undergraduate, you can begin considering what area of librarianship you wish to pursue, and focus on those courses. Many library schools don't require specific undergraduate courses for acceptance, but a good academic record and reading knowledge of at least one foreign language is usually required. You should also consider taking classes that strengthen your skills in communications, writing, research methods, collection organization, and customer service, as well as maintenance and conservation. More than half of the accredited library schools do not require any introductory courses in library science while an undergraduate. It would be wise, though, to check with schools for specific requirements.

Upon receiving your bachelor's degree, you will need to earn a master's degree to become a librarian. The degree is generally known as the master of library science (M.L.S), but in some institutions it may be referred to by a different title, such as the master of library and information science (M.L.I.S.). You should plan to attend a graduate school of library and information science that is accredited by the American Library Association (ALA). Currently, there are nearly 50 ALA-accredited schools. Some libraries do not consider job applicants who attended a nonaccredited school. Visit http://www.ala.org/ala/educationcareers/education/accreditedprograms/directory for a list of ALA-accredited programs.

During your one- or two-year graduate study program, you will take courses in reference work, cataloging, classification, computers, library organizations, and administration. Other courses focus on the history of books and printing and on issues of censorship and intellectual freedom. Information scientists focus on courses in computer sciences, mathematics, and systems analysis. Many library schools have work-study programs where students take classes while gaining practical experience in a library.

Specialized librarians, such as law, pharmaceutical, or geology librarians, must have a very strong background in the subject in which they wish to work. Most have a degree in their subject specialization in addition to their M.L.S. In some cases, a graduate or professional degree in the subject is especially attractive to prospective employers. For work in research libraries, university libraries, or special collections, a doctorate may be required. A doctorate is commonly required for the top administrative posts of these types of libraries, as well as for faculty positions in graduate schools of library science.

Certification or Licensing

In many states, school librarians are required to earn teacher's certification in addition to preparation as a librarian. They may also be required to earn a master's degree in education. Various state, county, and local governments have set up other requirements for education and certification. You should contact the school board in the area in which you are interested in working for specific requirements. Your public library system should also have that information readily available.

The ALA offers the certified public library administrator designation to public librarians who have at least three years of supervisory experience. For more information, visit http://ala-apa.org/certification.

Other Requirements

Librarians are often expected to take part in community affairs, cooperating in the preparation of exhibits, presenting book reviews, and explaining library use to community organizations. You will need to be a leader in developing the cultural tastes of the library patrons. Librarians who deal with the public should have strong interpersonal skills, tact, and patience. An imaginative, highly motivated, and resourceful personality is very valuable. An affinity for problem solving is another desirable quality. Library specialists, too, must have particular personal qualifications; for example, young-adult librarians must have a real liking for teenagers, and bookmobile librarians should feel comfortable traveling to outlying areas and dealing with all sorts of people.

Librarians involved with technical services should be detail oriented, have good planning skills, and be able to think analytically. All librarians should have a love for information and be willing to master the techniques for obtaining and presenting knowledge. They must also be prepared to master constantly changing technology.

EXPLORING

There are several ways you can explore the field of librarianship. First of all, high school students have their own personal experiences with the library: reading, doing research for class projects, or just browsing. If this experience sparks an interest in library work, you can talk with a school or community librarian whose own experiences in the field can provide a good idea of what goes on behind the scenes. Some schools may have library clubs you can join to learn about library work. If one does not exist, you could consider starting your own library club.

You can also learn more about library science by reading periodicals about the field such as *Library Journal* (http://www.library journal.com) and *American Libraries* (http://americanlibraries magazine.org).

Once you know you are interested in library work, you might be able to work as an assistant in the school library media center or find part-time work in a local public library. Such volunteer or paid positions may provide you with experience checking materials in and out at the circulation desk, shelving returned books, or typing title, subject, and author information on cards or in computer records. In college, you might be able to work as a technical or clerical assistant in one of your school's academic libraries.

The ALA provides a wealth of career information at its Web site, LibraryCareers.org (http://www.ala.org/ala/educationcareers/careers/librarycareerssite/home.cfm). Contact the ALA or another professional organization to inquire about student memberships. For example, the ALA offers a membership options for college students and nonlibrarians who are "interested in participating in the work of the association." Most groups offer excellent mentoring opportunities as well. Finally, if you have an e-mail account, sign up for one or more of the listservs offered by these groups. A listserv is an e-mail list of professionals throughout the world who consult each other on special topics. ALA members monitor a number of listservs for members and nonmembers. By subscribing to a listserv, you can discover what matters concern professional librarians today. Before you post your own comment or query, however, be sure you know the rules and regulations created by the list's moderator and always be respectful of others.

EMPLOYERS

Approximately 159,900 librarians are employed in the United States. All types of libraries need library professionals. Public libraries, school libraries, library media centers, college or university libraries, research libraries, and other special libraries all employ librarians. Private industry and government departments have libraries that need staffing. Librarians also work outside of the traditional library setting.

A librarian can work for a small branch office of a major library, or in a large library that services many counties. A librarian in a smaller library may have duties in all areas of librarianship: ordering, cataloging, shelving, and circulating materials, as well as acting as reference librarian. On the other hand, a librarian at a larger institution has more specialized duties, such as overseeing a history section or map room.

Many universities have multiple libraries that serve different groups of people. The University of Chicago library system, for example, has a separate law library; a general reading collection library; a mathematics, statistics, and computer science library; a humanities, social sciences, and business library; a science, medicine, and technology library; a social welfare and social work library; and a special collections research center. Librarians at such an institution might work in administration overseeing the branches of the entire system, or may deal with operations in one of the satellite areas.

Businesses and organizations also employ library professionals. *Special librarians* manage libraries for businesses, nonprofit corporations, and government agencies. The materials collected usually pertain to subjects of particular interest to the organization. (For more information, see the article "Corporate Librarians.") *Institution librarians* plan and direct library programs for residents and staff of institutions such as prisons, hospitals, and other extended-care facilities.

As the field of library and information services grows, librarians can find more work outside of the traditional library setting. Experienced information scientists may advise libraries or other agencies on information systems, library renovation projects, or other information-based issues. In addition, librarians act as *trainers* and *service representatives* for online database vendors, helping users access the information from online services.

STARTING OUT

Generally, librarians must complete all educational requirements before applying for a job. In some cases part-time work experience while in graduate school may turn into a full-time position upon graduation. Some employers, too, may allow an especially promising applicant to begin learning on the job before the library degree is conferred.

Upon graduating, new librarians should consult the career services office at their school. Employers seeking new graduates often recruit through library schools. Most professional library and information science organizations have job listings that candidates can consult. The ALA job Web site, http://joblist.ala.org, for example, offers links to employment opportunities throughout the country, as posted by different library organizations. The ALA also offers a career guidance Web site, http://www.getajob.ala.org, that provides tips on landing a job. Other useful library-related job-search and career resource sites include LisJobs.com (http://lisjobs.com) and Library Job Postings on the Internet (http://www.libraryjob postings.org).

Also, many online job search engines can help librarians find an appropriate position. Newspaper classifieds may be of some help in locating a job, although other approaches may be more appropriate to the profession.

Many librarians entering the workforce today are combining their experience in another career with graduate library and information science education. For example, a music teacher who plays trumpet in a band could mix her part-time teaching experience and her hobby with a degree in library science to begin a full-time career as a music librarian. Almost any background can be used to advantage when entering the field of librarianship.

Since school library media specialists work in grammar schools and high schools, they must apply directly to school boards. Individuals interested in working in library positions for the federal government can contact the human resources department—or consult the Web site of the government agency where they are interested in working; for these government positions, applicants must take a civil service examination. Public libraries, too, are often under a civil service system of appointment.

ADVANCEMENT

The beginning librarian may gain experience by taking a job as an assistant. He or she can learn a lot from practical experience before attempting to manage a department or entire library. A librarian may advance to positions with greater levels of responsibility within the same library system, or a librarian may gain initial experience in a small library and then advance by transferring to a larger or more specialized library. Within a large library, promotions to higher positions are possible, for example, to the supervision of a department. Experienced librarians with the necessary qualifications may advance to positions in library administration. A doctorate is desirable for reaching top administrative levels, as well as for taking a graduate library school faculty position.

Experienced librarians, in particular those with strong administrative, computer, or planning backgrounds, may move into the area of information consulting. They use their expertise to advise libraries and other organizations on issues regarding information services. Other experienced librarians, especially those with computer experience, may also go into specialized areas of library work, becoming increasingly valuable to business and industry, as well as other fields.

EARNINGS

Salaries depend on such factors as the location, size, and type of library, the amount of experience the librarian has, and the responsibilities of the position. According to the U.S. Department of Labor (DOL), median annual earnings of librarians were $53,710 in 2009. Salaries ranged from less than $33,480 to more than $82,450. Librarians working in elementary and secondary schools earned $57,950 in 2009 and those in colleges and universities earned about $59,430. Librarians employed in local government earned $49,920. In the federal government, the average salary for all librarians was about $79,550.

The American Library Association's Survey of Librarian Salaries reports the following mean salaries for librarians and managers in 2010: library directors/deans/chief officers, $99,176; deputy/associate/assistant directors, $79,274; department heads/senior managers, $65,829; managers/supervisors of support staff, $55,050; librarians who do not supervise, $53,923; and beginning librarians, $48,317.

Most librarians receive a full benefits package, which may include paid vacation time, holiday pay, compensated sick leave, various insurance plans, and retirement savings programs. Librarians who work in a college or university library may receive tuition waivers in order to earn advanced degrees in their field.

WORK ENVIRONMENT

Nearly all libraries are clean, comfortable, and pleasant places to work. Although libraries are typically quiet, they are hives of activity as librarians work with patrons and behind the scenes to provide services in a timely and efficient manner. Some librarians, such as reference or special librarians, may find the work demanding and stressful when they deal with users who are working under deadline pressure. Librarians working in technical services may suffer eyestrain and headaches from working long hours at the computer.

Librarians work between 35 and 40 hours per week. Since most libraries are open evenings and weekends to accommodate the schedules of their users, many librarians will have a nontraditional work schedule, working, for instance, from 11:00 A.M. to 9:00 P.M., or taking Monday and Tuesday as a weekend in lieu of Saturday and Sunday. Library media specialists usually work the same hours and have the same vacation schedule as teachers in the school system. Grade school or high school librarians may have shorter workdays or workweeks while school is out of session. Librarians working for the government or as special librarians usually work a 40-hour week during normal business hours. However, more and more librarians are finding it difficult to find full-time positions and are working in part-time positions instead. Approximately 25 percent of librarians work part time.

There is, of course, some routine in library work, but the trend is to place clerical duties in the hands of library technicians and library assistants, freeing the professional librarian for administrative, research, personnel, and community services. For the most part, librarians tend to find the work intellectually stimulating, challenging, and dynamic. The knowledge that one is providing so many valuable services to the community can be extremely rewarding.

OUTLOOK

Employment for librarians is expected to grow about as fast as the average for all careers through 2018, according to the DOL. A large number of librarians are expected to retire in the next decade, which will create favorable employment conditions. Despite this prediction, school and community libraries will be faced with escalating materials costs, tighter budgets, and increased circulation while having to rely more heavily on volunteers, part-time employees, and support staff. In some cases, libraries will hire a technician instead of a more highly paid librarian as a result of budget cuts. Librarians who are willing to relocate to states or districts facing fewer budget issues will have better employment opportunities.

Employment opportunities will be best in nontraditional library settings, such as information brokering companies, private corporations, and consulting firms. The outlook is good for those skilled in developing computerized library systems as well as for those with a strong command of one or more foreign languages.

The expanding use of computers to store and retrieve information and to handle routine operations will require that librarians have strong computer skills, and in some cases these tasks, once performed solely by librarians, can now be performed by other library staff members. However, the automation of libraries will in no way replace librarians; personal judgment and knowledge will always be needed in libraries.

Employment opportunities will also arise for librarians who have a background in information science and library automation. The rapidly expanding field of information management has created a demand for qualified people to set up and maintain information systems for private industry and consulting firms. Many companies are also establishing in-house reference libraries to assist in research work. Some have developed full lending library systems for employees.

Many librarians will find employment as trainers, customer representatives, and sales representatives for information database vendors. The expansion of the Internet will create new occupational opportunities for librarians—opportunities with such titles as database specialist, webmaster, Web developer, Internet trainer, Internet consultant, and Internet coordinator.

FOR MORE INFORMATION

For information on careers in law librarianship, contact
American Association of Law Libraries
105 West Adams Street, Suite 3300
Chicago, IL 60603-6225
Tel: 312-939-4764
http://www.aallnet.org

For career information and a list of accredited educational programs, contact
American Association of School Librarians
c/o American Library Association
50 East Huron Street
Chicago, IL 60611-2795
Tel: 800-545-2433, ext. 4382
E-mail: aasl@ala.org
http://www.ala.org/ala/mgrps/divs/aasl

For a list of accredited schools and information on careers, scholarships and grants, and membership, contact
American Library Association
50 East Huron Street
Chicago, IL 60611-2729
Tel: 800-545-2433
http://www.ala.org

To learn more about information science careers, contact
American Society for Information Science and Technology
1320 Fenwick Lane, Suite 510
Silver Spring, MD 20910-3560
Tel: 301-495-0900
E-mail: asis@asis.org
http://www.asis.org

For information on membership, contact
Asian Pacific American Librarians Association
PO Box 1669
Goleta, CA 93116-1669
http://www.apalaweb.org

For more information on careers in this field, contact
Association for Library Collections and Technical Services
50 East Huron Street
Chicago, IL 60611-2795
Tel: 800-545-2433, ext. 5037
E-mail: alcts@ala.org
http://www.ala.org/ala/mgrps/divs/alcts

For information on a career as a children's librarian, contact
Association for Library Service to Children
c/o American Library Association
50 East Huron Street
Chicago, IL 60611-2729
Tel: 800-545-2433, ext. 2163
E-mail: alsc@ala.org
http://www.ala.org/ala/mgrps/divs/alsc

For information on employment in academic settings, contact
Association of Academic Health Sciences Libraries
2150 North 107th Street, Suite 205

Seattle, WA 98133-9009
Tel: 206-367-8704
E-mail: aahsl@sbims.com
http://www.aahsl.org

For information on employment in academic settings, contact
Association of College and Research Libraries
c/o American Library Association
50 East Huron Street
Chicago, IL 60611-2795
Tel: 800-545-2433, ext. 2523
E-mail: acrl@ala.org
http://www.ala.org/ala/mgrps/divs/acrl

For information on employment in research settings, contact
Association of Research Libraries
21 Dupont Circle, NW, Suite 800
Washington DC 20036-1543
Tel: 202-296-2296
http://www.arl.org

For information on membership, contact
Chinese American Librarians Association
http://www.cala-web.org

For information on continuing education programs and publications, contact
Library & Information Technology Association
c/o American Library Association
50 East Huron Street
Chicago, IL 60611-2795
Tel: 800-545-2433, ext. 4270
E-mail: lita@ala.org
http://www.lita.org/ala/mgrps/divs/lita/index.cfm

For information on careers in medical librarianship, contact
Medical Library Association
65 East Wacker Place, Suite 1900
Chicago, IL 60601-7246
Tel: 312-419-9094
E-mail: info@mlahq.org
http://www.mlanet.org

For information on careers in music librarianship, contact
Music Library Association
8551 Research Way, Suite 180
Middleton, WI 53562-3567
Tel: 608-836-5825
E-mail: mla@areditions.com
http://www.musiclibraryassoc.org

The association is a membership organization for media technology centers.
National Association of Media and Technology Centers
PO Box 9844
Cedar Rapids, IA 52409-9844
Tel: 319-654-0608
http://www.namtc.org

To read Careers in Public Librarianship, *visit*
Public Library Association
c/o American Library Association
50 East Huron Street
Chicago, IL 60611-2795
Tel: 800-545-2433, ext. 5752
http://www.ala.org/ala/mgrps/divs/pla

For information on working in a specialized library, contact
Special Libraries Association
331 South Patrick Street
Alexandria, VA 22314-3501
Tel: 703-647-4900
http://www.sla.org

For information on the field of competitive intelligence, contact
Strategic and Competitive Intelligence Professionals
1700 Diagonal Road, Suite 600
Alexandria, VA 22314-2863
Tel: 703-739-0696
E-mail: info@scip.org
http://www.scip.org

For career information about librarians who provide services to students ages 12–18, visit
Young Adult Library Services Association
c/o American Library Association

50 East Huron Street
Chicago, IL 60611-2795
Tel: 800-545-2433, ext. 4390
E-mail: YALSA@ala.org
http://www.ala.org/ala/mgrps/divs/yalsa/yalsa.cfm

To receive information on librarianship in Canada, contact
Canadian Library Association
1150 Morrison Drive, Suite 400
Ottawa, ON K2H 8S9 Canada
Tel: 613-232-9625
E-mail: info@cla.ca
http://www.cla.ca

━━━━━━ INTERVIEW ━━━━━━

Karen Danczak Lyons is the first deputy commissioner of the Chicago Public Library. She discussed her career and the field of library and information science with the editors of Careers in Focus: Library and Information Science.

Q. How long have you worked in the field? What made you want to enter this career?

A. The library has always been an important part of my life. In both grammar school and high school I worked as a volunteer in the school libraries.

In 1993, Mayor Daley asked me to become the acting commissioner of the Chicago Public Library (CPL). Along with my handpicked team of management professionals we began to review, revise, and improve management practices at CPL.

In 1995, I began the master's in library and information science program at Rosary College (now Dominican University). I graduated from the program in January 1997 with honors.

When I joined the staff of the CPL, I felt as if I had come home. The mission and values of the public library align with my own, including public service, freedom, open access to information, and problem solving through information seeking.

Q. What are the most important personal and professional qualities for librarians?

A. To be a successful librarian, an individual must first enjoy working with people from all backgrounds and at many levels of ability. Practicing good communication skills is also critical—whether creating search queries, assisting with a reference interview through careful questioning and careful listening, or marketing library programs, the key to success is good communication. Of course, my list would not be complete without the following attributes: humor, flexibility, energy, curiosity, stamina, integrity, attention to detail, good problem-solving skills, and passion about the core mission of the profession.

Q. What are some of the pros and cons of your job?

A. "Variety is the spice of life" certainly applies to the library profession. No two days are the same, though each day provides opportunities to interact with interesting people, learn new things, and laugh. As demand for library service increases, staff members frequently wish for more time to assist patrons individually, but must find sources and offer assistance quickly and follow up as time permits.

Q. What advice would you give to young people who are interested in the field?

A. The field of librarianship allows an individual to follow his or her passion and constantly feed a curious mind. Whether your interest is in working with young students (school library media specialist); medical professionals, corporations, or lawyers (special librarians); university staff and students (academic librarians); or the public, there is an area of concentration for everyone. Of course, library specialties in technology and databases or preservation and the archival of materials are exciting options as well.

Q. What is the employment outlook for librarians? How is the field changing?

A. With the growth in technology, some traditional areas (cataloging of materials) are rapidly being automated. Book ordering is done much more efficiently online. All of the technology and comprehensive databases and search engines will never replace the need for the expertise of a degreed librarian. With the proliferation of data, access to someone trained in the organization of knowledge, equipped with superior searching skills and critical thinking, is the key to success. Now, more than ever, we need excited, curious new members of the library profession.

Library Assistants

QUICK FACTS

School Subjects
Computer science
English

Personal Skills
Following instructions
Helping/teaching

Work Environment
Primarily indoors
Primarily one location

Minimum Education Level
Some postsecondary training

Salary Range
$16,000 to $22,980 to
$37,070+

Certification or Licensing
Voluntary

Outlook
About as fast as the average

DOT
100, 249

GOE
12.03.04

NOC
5211

O*NET-SOC
43-4121.00

OVERVIEW

From sorting to stacking to swiping, *library assistants* keep books, periodicals, and other resource materials organized and easily accessible. Don't let the job title fool you; these professionals are critical in helping libraries, media centers, research facilities, and other information-based organizations run smoothly and effectively. There are approximately 122,000 library assistants working in the United States. Library assistants may also be known as *library aides, library technical assistants, media aides, library media assistants,* and *circulation assistant library clerks.*

HISTORY

Ancient private libraries date back to 3000 B.C., and the first U.S. institutional library dates back to the mid-1600s. With advanced printing technology and higher literacy rates, people soon were clamoring for books, and the concept of a public library where materials could be lent and borrowed was born. Books were no longer only in the hands of the wealthy, they were meant to be shared with greater civilization—and shared they were, so much to an extent that main library staff couldn't keep up with the work. They needed additional help to sort and reshelve books quickly, assist the public in finding and checking out books, and keeping books and other materials in good condition. Enter the library assistant.

Modern libraries today need assistants more than ever. With media technology shifting from the printed word to digital data storage, library assistants are also needed to assist in organizing and sorting electronic files in addition to traditional books and hard copy material.

THE JOB

Library assistants assist head librarians, research assistants, and other library staff in organizing materials and helping the public find the information they need. They may work in the checkout area, scanning books in and out of the library. They also may work in the shelves, pushing carts of returned and misshelved books and other material around and putting items back into their proper place. They may specialize in electronic media, helping to organize CD-ROMs, microfiches, DVDs, and other materials and make them accessible to library patrons. They manage and update electronic databases and library Web sites.

Much of library assistants' work will depend on the type of institution in which they are employed. In a large public library, they might work in a variety of areas or be staffed in one area such as circulation or the children's library. In a research or medical library, assistants need to be knowledgeable about the specific material kept in the institution and more importantly, how to find it. Assistants might also be mobile, working in outreach libraries or bookmobiles, helping to bring resources to remote areas and communities.

In addition to checking materials in and out of the library, assistants also prepare and repair books so that they are suitable for lending. They may affix card pockets and barcodes to materials and also place protective book covers—usually made of a thin, but durable plastic—on all books and periodicals. Compact discs, records, and other irregularly sized items must also be prepared for the shelves and protected from the wear and tear that comes with constant handling.

Assistants that work in circulation stamp due dates on materials and collect fines for overdue items. They scan the patron's library card to make sure no items are overdue and then assign new materials to the card. Most modern libraries have computer systems that track due dates of books and help library assistants locate individuals who have past due items. Library assistants mail notices to people who rack up large fines and collect smaller fines from patrons in person. These financial duties are crucial to helping the library remain financially sound and able to invest in more books and care for those already in the collection.

Some library assistants known as *braille-and-talking-books clerks* help those who are blind or visually impaired use library resources.

A library assistant (*right*) and a library director discuss an electronic system that manages cataloging, circulation, acquisitions, and other library tasks. *(S. Cannerelli, Syracuse Newspapers/The Image Works)*

They locate large-type or braille volumes and books on tape and give or mail them to the borrower.

All library assistants report to head and departmental librarians. All tasks are delegated to the assistants by these supervisors.

REQUIREMENTS

High School

Library assistants need strong English, history, speech, and even foreign language skills, so while in high school concentrate on the humanities. If you are interested in working in a special library such as a medical library, take classes in that specialty. Learning how to use a computer and conduct basic research in a library is essential. Developing these skills will not only aid in your future library work, but will also help you in college and in any other career options you might pursue.

Postsecondary Training

While little postsecondary training is required for an assistant job, the position is often a stepping-stone to a higher library position. If this is your end goal, you will need to work toward a master's degree in library science. The assistant job will give you wonderful on-the-job training. This coupled with education in the communications, writing, research methods, collection organization, and customer service, as well as maintenance and conservation will put you in a great position to land a librarian position. More than half of the accredited library schools do not require any introductory courses in library science while an undergraduate, but check with schools for specific requirements.

Certification or Licensing

The American Library Association (ALA) offers the voluntary library support staff certification designation to library support staff who demonstrate their knowledge and skills in library science. Library support staff with at least a high school diploma or its equivalent and at least one year of full-time experience in a library may apply for certification. Visit http://ala-apa.org/lssc for more information.

Various state, county, and local governments have established other requirements for education and certification. You should contact the school board in the area in which you are interested in working for specific requirements. Your public library system should also have that information readily available.

Other Requirements

Library assistants need to be organized, detailed oriented, and personable to work with the public. Tact and patience can come in handy when working on projects and assisting patrons with "strong personalities." An affinity for problem solving is another desirable quality. Depending on where they work, assistants should have the qualities to fit their place of work; for example those working at a children's or young adult library should be able to relate to people from these age groups and enjoy helping them and promoting literacy.

Assistants employed in technical services should be comfortable working with the technology needed for the job and be able to think analytically. Anyone who works in a library should have a love for information and a desire to master the techniques for obtaining and presenting knowledge. They must also be prepared to master constantly changing technology.

EXPLORING

While in high school, spend a good amount of time in your school or public library. Take notice of how materials are organized and handled from drop off to pick up. Just using your own library for school projects or perusing the aisles for new books will increase your knowledge of how libraries are organized and kindle your love for information. You may even want to ask if you can work part time in your school or public library as an assistant. Even just working on a volunteer basis will give you great experiences, including checking materials in and out at the circulation desk, working with patrons, shelving returned books, and working with book records.

The ALA and other professional organizations (listed at the end of this chapter) offer information on careers, education, and college student memberships. Be sure to explore what these associations have to offer.

EMPLOYERS

Library assistants hold approximately 122,000 jobs in the United States, with about 61 percent working part time. They work in public libraries, school libraries, library media centers, college or university libraries, research libraries, and other special libraries. Assistants in smaller libraries may have duties in all areas of librarianship: cataloging, shelving, and circulating materials, as well as assisting customers in locating materials. Conversely, an assistant at a large public or educational institution will probably work in a single area or floor of the library, concentrating on the materials kept only there, such as legal materials, audiovisual items and equipment, or music.

Businesses and organizations also employ library professionals. Assistants working for these employers may work in corporate libraries, nonprofit corporations, and government agencies, helping people find items of particular interest to the organization.

STARTING OUT

The position of library assistant is a perfect starting job in the library field. It offers those interested in career advancement the opportunity to explore different areas of the library to determine the area in which they want to work.

To find an assistant job, focus on larger institutions first because the need for assistants will be greater. Smaller facilities might only hire librarians, who handle all the administrative and professional tasks. Newspaper classifieds may be of some help in locating a job, although dropping by libraries with a resume might be more effective and direct.

Many library assistants work part time, combining work with school or even another job. For example, a music teacher who plays trumpet in a band could mix her part-time teaching experience and her interest in books and learning with part-time work in the school library. Almost any background can be used to advantage when entering the field of library science.

Since school library assistants work in grammar schools and high schools, they must apply directly to school boards. Individuals interested in working in library positions for the federal government can contact the human resources department—or consult the Web site of the government agency for which they are interested in working; applicants must take a civil service examination for government positions. Public libraries, too, are often under a civil service system of appointment.

ADVANCEMENT

Since the job of assistant is an entry-level job, there are many directions in which an individual can advance. From there, assistants can advance to any librarian position depending on their area of interest. Staff may advance to positions with greater levels of responsibility within the same library system, or they may gain initial experience in a small library and then advance by transferring to a larger or more specialized library. Within a large library, promotions to higher positions are possible, such as the supervision of a department.

EARNINGS

Salaries depend on such factors as the location, size, and type of library, the amount of experience the library assistant has, and the responsibilities of the position. According to the U.S. Department of Labor (DOL), the median annual salary of full-time library assistants was $22,980 in 2009. Salaries ranged from less than $16,000 to $37,070 or more. On average, assistants working in specialty libraries that require technical knowledge have higher earning potential.

Library assistants who work part time are paid hourly and generally do not receive benefits or paid vacation time. Because of this, many work at other jobs or go to school to advance in the profession.

Benefits for full-time workers include vacation and sick time, health, and sometimes dental, insurance, and pension or 401(k) plans. Part-time library assistants must provide their own benefits.

WORK ENVIRONMENT

Most libraries are pleasant and comfortable places in which to assist those doing research, studying, or reading for pleasure. Library assistants must do a considerable amount of reading to keep informed in order to serve library patrons. They must also strive to stay abreast of constantly changing technology, which may seem overwhelming at times.

Much of the job is considered "desk job" work. Assistants in reference or circulation may suffer eyestrain and headaches from working long hours in front of a computer screen.

Full-time assistants work between 35 and 40 hours per week, but part-time workers log only about 20 hours or less a week. Since most libraries are open evenings and weekends, staff must be available to work a nontraditional schedule, taking, for instance, an 11:00 A.M. to 9:00 P.M. shift or taking Monday and Tuesday as a weekend in lieu of Saturday and Sunday.

The nature of the work can be routine and therefore tedious. It can also be solitary and quiet if the assistant is working in the stacks. For the most part, however, these workers enjoy the environment and find the work intellectually stimulating, challenging, and dynamic. The ability to store, track, and share information with the public can be very rewarding.

OUTLOOK

Employment for library assistants is expected to grow about as fast as the average for all careers through 2018, according to the DOL. Job growth is expected to be strongest in special libraries. Many of the jobs once handled by librarians, such as checking books in and out and re-shelving and organizing materials, are now being delegated to assistants and technicians. This should increase demand for these positions. Part-time positions have high turnover and are, therefore, easy to find. This reflects the limited investment in training involved and the corresponding weak attachment to the occupation by part-time workers. Full-time assistant positions are rare. Big metropolitan areas offer more opportunities for employment than smaller, rural areas. Like other fields, the more eager an individual is to learn and stay up-to-date with current technology, the greater his or her chances of finding employment.

FOR MORE INFORMATION

For information on careers in law librarianship, contact
American Association of Law Libraries
105 West Adams Street, Suite 3300
Chicago, IL 60603-6225
Tel: 312-939-4764
http://www.aallnet.org

For a list of accredited schools and information on careers, certification, scholarships and grants, and membership, contact
American Library Association
50 East Huron Street
Chicago, IL 60611-2729
Tel: 800-545-2433
http://www.ala.org

To learn more about information science careers, contact
American Society for Information Science and Technology
1320 Fenwick Lane, Suite 510
Silver Spring, MD 20910-3560
Tel: 301-495-0900
E-mail: asis@asis.org
http://www.asis.org

For information on library support education and careers, contact
Council on Library/Media Technicians
PO Box 42048 Mesa, AZ 85274-2048
http://colt.ucr.edu

For information on careers in medical librarianship, contact
Medical Library Association
65 East Wacker Place, Suite 1900
Chicago, IL 60601-7246
Tel: 312-419-9094
E-mail: info@mlahq.org
http://www.mlanet.org

For information on careers in music librarianship, contact
Music Library Association
8551 Research Way, Suite 180
Middleton, WI 53562-3567
Tel: 608-836-5825
E-mail: mla@areditions.com
http://www.musiclibraryassoc.org

For information on working in a specialized library, contact
Special Libraries Association
331 South Patrick Street
Alexandria, VA 22314-3501
Tel: 703-647-4900
http://www.sla.org

For information on librarianship in Canada, contact
Canadian Library Association
1150 Morrison Drive, Suite 400
Ottawa, ON K2H 8S9 Canada
Tel: 613-232-9625
E-mail: info@cla.ca
http://www.cla.ca

—— INTERVIEW ——

Linda Blum and Mary Campbell are acquisition specialists/library assistants in the Technical Services Department at a public library in a major city in Wisconsin. Linda has worked full time at the library for 37 years and in the Technical Services Department for about 31 years. Mary has been an employee of the library for 28 years, with the last six years spent working in the Technical Services Department. Linda's and Mary's jobs are to order materials for the library—the books, magazine subscriptions, DVDs, CDs, Play-aways, etc.—for the public to use. As part of the acquisitions work, they review materials when they arrive, confirming exactly what was sent. Linda and Mary discussed their careers and the field of library and information science with the editors of Careers in Focus: Library and Information Science.

Q. What do you like most and least about your jobs?
A. *Linda:* With technology constantly changing, you always get to learn new ways to do things. You have to think and pay attention with this job and that keeps it interesting. I can't think of many cons. I know some people wouldn't like this job because you don't get to work with the public. But I prefer doing this type of work.

Mary: One pro related to technology is that we do more and more work online and store information in the computer database. So we use a lot less paper than we used to, and that makes me feel good. There's less waste. The only con I can think of is that the amount of work can get overwhelming sometimes, depending on where you are in the fiscal year. For example, in November and December, when it's the end of the budget year, everyone wants to have the last of their orders in and delivered so that when they start the new fiscal year, they won't still need to pay for things from last year. Times like that can get a little hectic. However, while it may sound like the daily work is repetitive, there's also a lot of flexibility within that framework because there are so many different things to do. I never do the same thing all day, and that's a big plus to me.

Q. What are the most important personal and professional qualities for acquisition specialists/library assistants?

A. *Linda:* Someone who is good with numbers and details would do well at this job. After all, you are working with a budget of several hundred thousand dollars and you're responsible for everything matching up. Accuracy is also important. This is a job for someone who likes to keep track of things.

Mary: You don't need an accounting degree, but it helps to know something about accounting procedures. Honesty is important, too. And you should have a cooperative personality, be a team player. You have to work with other people in your department as well as people in other departments and the vendors. So you need to be able to get along with people.

Q. What advice would you give to young people who are interested in the field?

A. *Linda:* Before I came into this department, I worked in every other department of the library. That gave me a really good understanding of how the library worked as a whole. So I suggest you try to get as much experience as you can in any library department. That will also help you decide what you like to do and what you don't. So get exposure to the different parts of the library.

There might be libraries around you where you could volunteer. When I was in high school, my youngest sister was going to grade school and I ended up volunteering at her school library. I got to do things like mend bookbindings, reshelve books, and help little kids find things. It was great.

You could also work on planning events for a club or group. Say you plan an outing or a party; you might have to decide how much money to spend, what supplies to get, and go buy them. You'd have to come up with a schedule and follow through, working with people in your group and outside of it. In the end, think about how everything went and what you might do differently next time and what you liked about the process.

Mary: Volunteering at a library is a good idea. Volunteering helps you find out what area of work you might like to do.

And you don't have to be a "bookworm" to do this job. When people learn I work at the public library, they often say to me, "You must get to read a lot." But I never read while I'm here.

Another way to explore this kind of work is to act as the treasurer for any groups or clubs that you might be in. That would give you exposure to working with budgets for an organization.

If you're already involved with a group, like 4-H or Girl Scouts, you could arrange for your group to take a tour of the public library. You'd be able to see the different areas and meet someone who has library work experience. You could also ask a local library director if he or she is willing to be interviewed about their work, or you could invite them to talk to your group. Many public library directors are happy to talk to people in their community about the library.

Q. What is the future employment outlook for library and information science?

A. *Linda*: Libraries are here to stay. And public libraries have to offer materials to the public. It doesn't matter if it's no longer paper books. Any type of material—e-books, Playaways, subscriptions to online magazines, and other text—they all have to be chosen and ordered and made available.

Mary: Acquisition specialists will be needed as long as there are libraries. So someone will always be needed to order the materials and make sure what comes in is correct.

Library Directors

OVERVIEW

Library directors, also referred to as *head librarians* or *library administrators*, manage libraries. Much of their work is administrative, for example, creating a budget for new book acquisitions and technological equipment, managing the library's collection, fund-raising, devising public relations campaigns, working with community or academic leaders, and hiring, training, and scheduling library staff.

HISTORY

In early libraries, librarians typically were responsible for administrative tasks, as well as their regular duties. But as libraries grew in size and complexity, it became apparent that managers were needed to hire, train, and oversee workers; prepare budgets; raise money for capital improvement projects; develop new outreach programs; manage the library's collection; and handle countless other tasks that librarians were too busy to address. Hence the career of library director was born.

Today, the rapid growth of computer- and Internet-based technology in libraries has created strong demand and new career challenges for library directors. The Library Administration and Management Association, a division of the American Library Association (ALA), was founded in 1957. It offers career development and support to library directors nationwide.

QUICK FACTS

School Subjects
Business
Computer science
English

Personal Skills
Helping/teaching
Leadership/management

Work Environment
Primarily indoors
Primarily one location

Minimum Education Level
Master's degree

Salary Range
$55,055 to $65,829 to $119,000+

Certification or Licensing
Voluntary

Outlook
About as fast as the average

DOT
100

GOE
12.03.04

NOC
0511

O*NET-SOC
25-4021.00

THE JOB

Library directors are the head of a library organization and are responsible for all library operations, such as planning and assessing the collection, staff development, and providing service to customers. They manage and help train employees working in reference, collection development, technical services, cataloging, circulation, and other areas of the library.

In addition to managing staff, library directors also must manage the various types of resources offered at the library: from CD-ROMs, to Internet information, to audio and video resources, to traditional media such as periodicals, magazines, and books. Directors set policies for circulation staff to carry out, such as signup systems for membership, record-keeping protocol, and the tracking of lost books.

Directors work with acquisition staff to help develop, maintain, and replace items in the library collection. The director must work within the boundaries of his or her predetermined budget and is the point person for any financial decisions within the library. Many directors seek out and write grants for financing new purchases above and beyond what tax dollars or school budgets can pay for and even seek out financial or book donations from community members to offset budget deficits.

Library directors work in four main types of libraries: public, school, academic, and specialty.

Public libraries range in size from the New York Public Library with millions of volumes and many branch libraries to town libraries with 10,000 to 15,000 volumes. *Public library directors* direct and manage the staff and operations of these community-based libraries. Their job is unique in that they must make sure information is made easily accessible to anyone who holds a library card: from the fourth-grade student who is working on a book report, to a parent researching college financing, to a senior looking to make the most of retirement. Public libraries must have a little something for everyone, and directors of these libraries must be familiar with all this information. There are approximately 9,221 public libraries in the United States.

School library directors oversee the operation of a library hosted within a school for student, faculty, and staff use. They work with their staff to help promote and encourage literacy and teach research skills so students can find information for school projects. There are about 99,180 libraries in elementary, junior high, and high schools.

Although the job of *academic library director* may sound similar to that of library directors working in school libraries, the career is actually quite different. Academic libraries are found in higher places of learning like universities, rather than a local elementary or high school. These libraries range from a 10,000-volume library to the many millions of volumes in large private and public

A library director (*right*) and a book conservator study a book that was restored after being damaged in a fire. *(Jens Meyer, AP Photo)*

university libraries. Their clientele ranges from beginning college freshmen to university professors engaged in research. Directors of these libraries oversee staff that document and store this important research and help students, professors, researchers, and other academics find and use this information. There are approximately 3,827 academic libraries of all types serving millions of students enrolled in institutions of higher education: junior colleges, colleges, and universities.

Special libraries provide specialized information services to trade organizations, research laboratories, businesses, government agencies, art museums, hospitals, newspapers, publishers, and others. Examples of special library collections might be a medical library in a hospital or a music library in a museum or at a record company. Most large corporations also have special libraries for employee use. The library of a pharmaceutical company, for example, may contain 10,000 to 15,000 volumes carefully selected to aid the scientists who carry on research and testing of new medicines. *Special library directors* manage the resources and employees in these libraries. There are approximately 8,476 special libraries.

Regardless of the type of library in which the director works, he or she must be able to wear many hats to ensure that the library is well used, well managed, and fiscally sound.

REQUIREMENTS

High School

Take English, business, mathematics, computer science, and foreign language to prepare for this career. Also, taking courses that require the writing of reports will help you hone your research and writing skills. Being a voracious reader will also be very helpful. You should become a media center aide at your school library to get valuable working experience while at the same time familiarizing yourself with the library.

Postsecondary Training

Undergraduate training will vary depending on the type of library career you choose to pursue. Many library directors, especially those employed in a reference library, have a bachelor's degree in education. If you plan to become a director of a special library, then it would be wise to earn an undergraduate degree in a related field. Directors of corporate libraries, for example, often have degrees in business. Those who manage a music library may have degrees in music.

All librarians, including library directors, must have a master's degree in library science (M.L.S.) or a master's degree in library and information science (M.L.I.S). Employers prefer to hire graduates of ALA-accredited programs. Visit the ALA Web site, http://www.ala .org/ala/educationcareers/education/accreditedprograms/directory to view a list of accredited schools. Programs last from one to two years. Typical classes might include Administrative Management of Library Information Centers, Human Resource Management in Libraries and Information Centers, Collection Development and Management, Information Technology in Library Management, and Management of Specialized Information Services. Larger libraries or university libraries require library directors to have a Ph.D. in library science or a related field.

Many library directors choose to continue their education by attending conferences, training seminars, and workshops. Continuing education classes keep library directors current with emerging trends in information services.

Certification or Licensing

The ALA offers the certified public library administrator designation to public librarians who have at least three years of supervisory experience. For more information, visit http://ala-apa.org/ certification.

Other Requirements

Library directors should have excellent organizational and financial management skills, be good communicators in order to be able to successfully interact with and manage employees, have a love of information, and be willing to continually learn about the field and new technologies.

EXPLORING

You can get a taste of what this job entails by volunteering or obtaining a part-time job at your local library or school library. Your duties will be clerical in nature—shelving books and periodicals, cleaning or organizing stacks, or working the circulation desk—but each task will give you valuable hands-on experience, as well as an opportunity to interact with library directors and other library professionals.

You can also learn more about library science by reading periodicals about the field such as *Library Journal* (http://www.library journal.com) and *American Libraries* (http://americanlibraries magazine.org).

Professional associations can also provide a wealth of information about this career. Check out the ALA career Web site, LibraryCareers.org (http://www.ala.org/ala/educationcareers/careers/librarycareerssite/home.cfm), for articles on different library careers and profiles of librarians already established in their fields. You may want to also participate in online discussion groups to get an insider's view of this industry. Additionally, people interested in libraries and the work of librarians can join the ALA via a personal membership.

EMPLOYERS

Library directors are employed at public, school, academic, and special libraries. Public, school, and academic libraries are located throughout the United States. Special libraries, such as an association library or medical library, tend to be located in large metropolitan areas, so you may have to relocate if you would like to become a special library director. Other library directors are employed in the armed forces.

STARTING OUT

The position of library director typically is not an entry-level career. Most employers require that director candidates have at least three to five years of library work experience at the administrative level to be eligible for a position. Aspiring library directors first gain experience as librarians or in lower-level administrative positions such as *chief librarian* or *associate director* before seeking promotion to the position of library director. Chief librarians manage branch libraries or individual departments, such as the general reference, children's, circulation, or music departments; periodical reading room; or readers' advisory service. Associate directors assist the director in the library's daily operations. They are often assigned their own projects to manage or may be responsible for a small staff.

ADVANCEMENT

Library directors have many opportunities for advancement. Some transfer to larger library systems or university libraries. Others choose to teach at the postsecondary level.

Many directors become *consultants* or *information brokers* and conduct research for corporations, associations, and private businesses on a per project basis. Many library professionals enjoy working as consultants because of the opportunity for nontraditional hours, the high pay, and flexibility regarding projects.

EARNINGS

The American Library Association's Survey of Librarian Salaries reports the following mean salaries for library managers in 2010: library directors/deans/chief officers, $99,176; deputy/associate/assistant directors, $79,274; department heads/senior managers, $65,829; and managers/supervisors of support staff, $55,055.

According to Salary.com, library directors in higher education had salaries that ranged from less than $67,835 to $119,000 or more in 2010.

Benefits for full-time library directors include compensated sick leave, paid vacation time, holiday pay, various insurance plans, and retirement savings programs.

WORK ENVIRONMENT

Library directors typically work a 40-hour workweek, though some weekend and evening hours may be required. School library directors typically have their work schedules tied to the academic calendar.

Library directors are expected to attend workshops, conferences, meetings, and some community events. At times the job can be very stressful, even more so when a director has to juggle multiple projects, face a big deadline, or deal with employees who are not meeting their expectations. Unlike other librarians, directors have little contact with library patrons. This is especially true in libraries with larger staffs.

OUTLOOK

The U.S. Department of Labor (DOL) predicts that employment of librarians will grow about as fast as the average for all careers through 2018. Many openings will arise as a result of a large number of librarians retiring in the next decade. Employment opportunities for qualified library directors should also be good. Although library directors will be in demand in a variety of library settings, the DOL predicts that opportunities for library professionals will be best in nontraditional settings such as private corporations, nonprofit organizations, and consulting firms. As always, library directors with the most education and experience will have the best employment opportunities.

FOR MORE INFORMATION

For information on careers in law librarianship, contact
American Association of Law Libraries
105 West Adams Street, Suite 3300
Chicago, IL 60603-6225
Tel: 312-939-4764
http://www.aallnet.org

For a list of accredited schools and information on careers, scholarships and grants, and membership, contact
American Library Association
50 East Huron Street
Chicago, IL 60611-2729
Tel: 800-545-2433
http://www.ala.org

To learn more about information science careers, contact
American Society for Information Science and Technology
1320 Fenwick Lane, Suite 510
Silver Spring, MD 20910-3560
Tel: 301-495-0900
E-mail: asis@asis.org
http://www.asis.org

For information on continuing education programs and publications, contact
Library & Information Technology Association
c/o American Library Association
50 East Huron Street
Chicago, IL 60611-2795
Tel: 800-545-2433, ext. 4270
E-mail: lita@ala.org
http://www.lita.org/ala/mgrps/divs/lita/index.cfm

For information on careers in library management, contact
Library Leadership and Management Association
c/o American Library Association
50 East Huron Street
Chicago, IL 60611-2795
Tel: 800-545-2433, ext. 5032
E-mail: lama@ala.org
http://www.ala.org/ala/mgrps/divs/llama

For information on careers in medical librarianship, contact
Medical Library Association
65 East Wacker Place, Suite 1900
Chicago, IL 60601-7246
Tel: 312-419-9094
E-mail: info@mlahq.org
http://www.mlanet.org

For information on careers in music librarianship, contact
Music Library Association
8551 Research Way, Suite 180
Middleton, WI 53562-3567
Tel: 608-836-5825
E-mail: mla@areditions.com
http://www.musiclibraryassoc.org

For information on working in a specialized library, contact
Special Libraries Association
331 South Patrick Street
Alexandria, VA 22314-3501
Tel: 703-647-4900
http://www.sla.org

For information on librarianship in Canada, contact
Canadian Library Association
1150 Morrison Drive, Suite 400
Ottawa, ON K2H 8S9 Canada
Tel: 613-232-9625
E-mail: info@cla.ca
http://www.cla.ca

INTERVIEW

James Lutz is the director of library administrative services at the Texas Christian University Library in Fort Worth, Texas. He discussed his career and the field of library and information science with the editors of Careers in Focus: Library and Information Science.

Q. How long have you worked in the field? What made you want to enter this career?

A. I received my M.S.L.S. from the University of Kentucky in 1996 and have been employed in librarianship as a librarian for the past 14 years. Prior to earning my M.S.L.S. I was employed for about 18 months at West Virginia University in a split position that allowed me to work four mornings in interlibrary loan, five afternoons in government documents with a map library emphasis, and one evening on the reference desk.

It was this diverse set of experiences that showed me that librarianship had many different components. This was also a time in which the Internet and HTML in specific was coming into its own. The ability to extend information beyond the four walls of a building was an exciting opportunity to organize information in new ways.

Q. Can you please describe a day in your life on the job?

A. As the director of library administrative services I have responsibilities for the library safety and security, student employment issues, management of the circulation department, publications and public relations, purchasing, liaison to the campus physical plant as a building deputy, and additional duties.

On any given day I have several meetings. Meetings can concern internal library decisions or can be broader and deal with campus, regional, or even national issues. Opportunity in a university setting allows for involvement in staff assembly or on a professional level with the American Library Association.

When not meeting, a portion of the day is devoted to routine tasks that enable a library to function—ordering supplies, turning in work orders and following up to ensure they are completed, and reconciling budgets and fulfilling paperwork obligations to ensure employees are hired and paid.

Another component of a typical day are the interruptive and reactive aspects. [These might include] responding to internal and external user needs; having a computer fan fail and jeopardize the ability of an automated audio/video distribution system to function; analyzing a problem with a compact shelving carriage and providing an employee the means to contact a company and request servicing so a portion of the collection can be accessed; working with multiple campus groups and an outside contractor to determine why a photocopier is not properly reporting revenue from the copier through the identification card center that collects the data and ultimately back to the library's revenue; or calling in a myriad of service orders dealing with everything from hot and cold complaints to backed-up toilets. These are just a few examples of what can happen in a single day that do not appear on a calendar at the beginning of the day.

Q. What are the most important personal and professional qualities for people in your career?

A. An ability to listen and communicate effectively in appropriate detail.

Q. What are some of the pros and cons of your job?

A. Pros are the moments in which the students, faculty, or staff are able to use the resources the library offers to further their learning process, and they share their joy and discovery with you. Cons can be the cyclical nature of the job.

Q. What advice would you give to young people who are interested in the field?

A. The profession of librarian has immense variety in what you can do and the role you choose to play. First and foremost, you need to get past whatever stereotypes you have built up about a library and a librarian. A doctor "heals people" is a pretty easy summation for the medical profession, but there are so many other aspects. Librarianship is about connecting people to information. While that is the basic statement, many have an impression that librarian equals book tender. Being a librarian is about connecting people and their needs to resources that further their learning into knowledge.

Q. What is the future employment outlook for library science? How is the field changing?

A. It is an exciting field. It's only constant at this time is change. In these changes opportunities abound. Information classification, organization, and dissemination are critical and vital now more than ever. Traditional librarian positions are evolving and, while the physical interaction between library user and librarian exists, there is now more need for librarians to understand and utilize the technology resources to meet the user at their virtual location rather than at the librarians' physical location.

Library Media
Specialists

QUICK FACTS

School Subjects
Computer science
English

Personal Skills
Communication/ideas
Helping/teaching

Work Environment
Primarily indoors
Primarily one location

Minimum Education Level
Master's degree

Salary Range
$33,480 to $53,710 to
$82,450+

Certification or Licensing
Required for certain
positions

Outlook
About as fast as the average

DOT
100

GOE
12.03.04

NOC
N/A

O*NET-SOC
25-4021.00, 25-9011.00

OVERVIEW

Library media specialists, sometimes called *librarian/media specialists, library media teachers, audiovisual specialists, audio-visual collections specialists, school media specialists*, or *school media center directors*, manage their organization's media center. They are school staff members who help teachers and students find and use the information available to them through print and audiovisual sources. They acquire and maintain their schools' resources, which may include cameras, slide and film projectors, overhead and opaque projectors, television and video equipment, recording equipment, computers, and compact disc and DVD players. They also acquire and maintain items, such as records, audio and video recordings, films, compact discs, DVDs, and CD-ROMs, that are used with the equipment. There are approximately 66,000 library media specialists employed in the United States.

HISTORY

In the past, fundamental teaching tools consisted of the classroom's books, maps, globes, and chalkboard. Educators in the early part of the 20th century began to realize that students and teachers needed more extensive, organized resource materials. Libraries in high schools developed first, and elementary schools developed their own libraries in the years after World War II. School librarians were frequently former teachers who made a midcareer change from running a classroom to running a library. As the number of school libraries grew and the need for librarians increased, more people began specializing in school librarianship as a primary career.

Traditionally, the school library contained mainly books and magazines. However, just as society itself has become more technological through the years—with the development of new methods of storing, organizing, and retrieving information—basic education principles have changed and developed. Even the name of the school library has changed to mirror these developments: Today, a school may have a library media center, a learning resource center, or an instructional materials center. Much more sophisticated equipment is now available to help teachers perform their jobs, as well. For instance, many schools have computers with CD-ROM and DVD drives and access to remote sources of information on the Internet, in addition to many other sophisticated pieces of audiovisual equipment. It has become necessary for schools to employ trained professionals who are familiar with the capabilities of this equipment, and so the role of the school librarian has evolved into the role of the library media specialist. These professionals help teachers perform today's more complex teaching tasks by either instructing the teachers or teaching the students how to function in an increasingly technological world.

THE JOB

Library media specialists may work in library media centers in elementary, middle, and high schools. Library media centers can be found in either public schools (and, as such, part of public school districts), private schools, parochial schools, or other nonpublic schools. The specific responsibilities of the library media specialist vary according to the size of the school or school district, the grade level of the students, and the extent to which the library media center has invested in new technologies. In any case, there are many facets to the job of a library media specialist. Library media specialists must act as information specialist, teacher, and instructional consultant.

In the role of information specialist, library media professionals select, organize, catalog, and provide the means of accessing information stored in numerous print and nonprint sources. Since they are responsible for acquiring the resources that exist in many different formats, library media specialists study manufacturers' literature, talk with salespeople, inspect new product lines, and attend professional conferences and conventions to help determine the best sources available to meet the needs of their particular school community. They must be familiar with the new technologies that are constantly developing, and they may be involved with the budgeting and planning needed to acquire these new technologies for the library media center.

Library media specialists also organize all of the resource material stored in the library media center. They assign numbers to each audiovisual aid stored in their media center, they maintain catalogs of software, and they keep schedules showing when teachers plan to use specific materials. They perform such simple maintenance work as cleaning lenses and changing light bulbs, and they call in skilled technicians for more complicated maintenance or repairs on audiovisual or computer equipment.

Ultimately, the library media specialist must be completely familiar with all of the information available in the library media center, as well as with the new technologies that have been adopted by the facility. They must be able to help others access all of the information available to them through resources such as CD-ROMs, DVDs, computer databases, and the Internet. In some cases, when particular sources are not available, they may use cameras, computers, and art supplies to make their own audiovisual materials.

In the role of teacher, library media specialists provide training in information literacy. By helping teachers and students to access information, a specialist may apply both formal and informal teaching procedures. They may instruct teachers in the use of different print materials or audiovisual equipment, or may even teach the teachers how to use basic computer programs in the classroom. Library media specialists may either instruct students in classes, in small groups, or on a one-to-one basis. In some situations they may team-teach with teachers. They help teachers and students to most effectively utilize all of the resources available in the media center, directing them to appropriate print sources and teaching them how to navigate the Internet and to use sources like online encyclopedias and information databases. They may also help teachers produce special materials for class projects.

In elementary schools, library media specialists may provide activities geared to the learning process of the younger student. For instance, they may plan activities, such as story hours and puppet shows, that are designed to encourage reading. They may also create a special reading room for the younger students—brightly decorated with characters from favorite children's books and made comfortable and cozy with bean bag chairs and big floor pillows—where children can take a break and foster their love of books.

In the role of instructional consultant, library media specialists assist in curriculum development, help teachers to plan classes, recommend appropriate media for classes, and order materials that teachers request. They must be familiar with the subjects that each grade studies, know how children learn, and understand what training aids are best for specific age levels and topics. In this role, library media specialists may participate in school committees or school district committees that plan and revise curricula. They may represent their school or school district at conventions for school media center librarians, and often belong to professional library associations.

REQUIREMENTS

High School

You should prepare for this field of library media by taking a strong college preparatory course load, including classes in English, science, foreign languages, history, geography, and mathematics. Additional study in communications, graphic arts, television, computers, and photography will give you good background knowledge of the materials you will use every day as a library media specialist. You may also consider taking courses in psychology, sociology, education, and child development to help you learn about the different age groups you will encounter in your profession, and how you can best help them in your role as a library media specialist. Computer science classes are also very important because they will help you learn more about technology and the Internet.

Postsecondary Training

After high school, you should earn an undergraduate degree in the liberal arts, educational media, or instructional technology. Depending on the major you choose, you will probably need to take courses in English, communications, speech, and computer science. All of these courses can further your expertise with the tools you will use as a media specialist. Additional studies in child development and education will prepare you for working with all age groups, and will make it easier for you to achieve teacher's certification when you are ready to begin working as a professional library media specialist.

Although some current library media specialists presently have only bachelor's degrees, the American Library Association (ALA) recommends that entry-level library media specialist positions require a master's degree in library and information science (M.L.I.S.) or a master's degree with a specialty in school library media, educational media, instructional technology, communications, or education. Certain master's programs that prepare for a specialization in school library media are accredited by the ALA or by the National Council for the Accreditation of Teacher Education. In a master's degree program, a typical course load would include courses in cataloging, reference sources, children's and young-adult literature, library automation, library-oriented computer technology, and media program management.

Certification or Licensing

Most states require that media specialists employed in public school systems have teaching certification. Many states require that they also have certification in library media from the National Board for Professional Teaching Standards (http://www.nbpts.org).

Individuals interested in specializing in the field of library media should become familiar with the specific educational and certification requirements of a particular state department of education if they plan to work in a public school. Since the different certification requirements from state to state may present problems for people who relocate, many states have set up reciprocity agreements. Under such agreements, individuals who have achieved certification in one state may be able to receive certification in another state, despite different requirements. Private, parochial, or other nonpublic schools often have less specific certification requirements for their school employees.

Other Requirements

Library media specialists must be creative, inventive, and adaptable. They should enjoy working with children and young adults, and they should be able to communicate well with many different people. They must be able to handle responsibility and to work well under pressure. Good organizational and planning skills are also very valuable. Media specialists must have good manual skills and the ability to work with machines and technology. They need to have the skills to operate different types of audiovisual equipment and the ability to teach others how to operate the equipment.

A commitment to learning is necessary to deal with constantly changing technology. The ability to understand and implement new library media technologies, as well as to teach others how to utilize new technologies, is invaluable.

EXPLORING

Your first opportunity to see what goes on in a library media center will be personal experience in an elementary or high school library media center. You may have the chance to take part in a class in which a library media specialist teaches you how to use the Internet

A library media specialist helps a student in the media center of a high school library. *(Jim West, The Image Works)*

to locate information. Or you may also work alone in the library media center, utilizing the various print or audiovisual sources to complete a school project. In these and many other cases, you will get an idea of the informational tools available in library media centers, as well as the responsibilities held by specialists in making sure that those tools are used effectively and efficiently.

If you are interested in becoming a media specialist, volunteer to work in your school media programs. Perhaps your school offers a library club for its students. You might also read books and periodicals that deal with visual aids and education, and try to find summer or part-time employment with stores that sell audiovisual aids or companies that produce audiovisual equipment or software. Student memberships in professional library organizations are often available (and affordable). If you are considering a career in librarianship, try contacting a professional librarian association. You may be able to join the organization, attend professional meetings, or to meet individually with librarians who can offer you advice on how you can learn more about this career.

EMPLOYERS

Approximately 66,000 library media specialists are employed in the United States. Public and private grammar schools that have library media centers will employ library media specialists to manage their collections. Specialists may also be called upon to help schools develop a school library center by acquiring materials and setting up the media center. High schools and college preparatory schools need library media specialists to help students and teachers access and learn to use materials in the centers.

Although the title library media specialist generally refers to a librarian who works in grammar schools or high schools, media specialists often find employment outside of the school system. They may work in the libraries of law firms, private corporations, museums, zoos, historical societies, community organizations, and special institutions. They may also find employment as advisers for developers of software, books, and other educational media for children and young adults.

STARTING OUT

Before applying for a position as a library media specialist in a public school system, librarians usually will have completed the educational and certification requirements set by their state board of education. Positions in nonpublic schools may not have such rigid requirements. You should contact the school district where you are interested in working for specific requirements.

Most graduate schools have career services offices that offer assistance to their students in finding jobs. Professional associations, such as the American Library Association and the American Association of School Librarians, offer the opportunity to network with professionals in the field, as well as job listings at their Web sites. Some schools advertise openings in professional or educational journals. Most openings in school library media centers occur at the end of the school year, when many incumbents retire, get promoted, or move on to other positions. Some beginning media specialists may be able to secure employment right before the school year begins as well, when many school boards are scrambling to fill positions before classes start.

As was the case in the early history of school libraries, school library media specialists often come to the position after having worked as teachers. If you are not sure if school library media is the field for you, but you know you want to work with children, consider studying to become a teacher first. This will give you a good background with children and their needs. Then, by taking additional classes on a part-time basis, you can meet the requirements needed in order to move from the classroom into the library media center.

ADVANCEMENT

Library media specialists may advance in their library media center to supervise various clerical personnel and volunteers. After having accumulated experience working directly with students and teachers, a specialist working in a school system may advance into the administrative realm, becoming media program coordinator for an entire school district. Experienced administrators, especially those who have pursued additional training, may eventually advance to become curriculum development superintendents.

Experienced library media specialists who earn a Ph.D. or an Ed.D. may find work as college instructors or directors of college media programs. Some media specialists find better paying positions by leaving the school setting and taking positions with companies that develop teaching aids. Others may use their skills to set up their own media product companies.

EARNINGS

The U.S. Department of Labor (DOL) does not provide salary information for library media specialists, but it does provide salary data for librarians (a category that includes library media specialists who have a master's degree in library and information science). Librarians had median annual earnings of $53,710 in 2009, according to the DOL. Ten percent earned less than $33,480, and 10 percent earned more than $82,450. Librarians working in elementary and secondary schools earned mean salaries of $57,950. Media specialists who act as a faculty adviser to student teams and clubs usually receive additional compensation.

Benefits for library media specialists usually include health insurance, sick leave, vacation time, and pension plans. Some schools may offer tuition assistance plans to help their employees earn advanced degrees. Most schools are closed for two to three months each summer, two to four weeks over the winter holidays, as well as various local, state, and national holidays. Often, school employees can choose to have their salary prorated so they can receive a paycheck year-round.

WORK ENVIRONMENT

Most library media specialists work in grade schools or high schools, and they usually work in library media centers that have facilities for previewing software, making audiovisual aids, and storing equipment. Specialists deal with students and teachers every day and often face frequent interruptions to answer questions or to provide instruction. Teachers often visit them to discuss materials they need for their classes, to look through media catalogs, and to see slides and films. Library media specialists are constantly busy checking orders and inspecting new products, and they are often responsible for large budgets.

In addition, as members of the school faculty, library media specialists often attend faculty meetings and serve as student advisers. They might also supervise extracurricular activities as a club adviser or team coach. They frequently work late, take work home, and go to meetings at night and on the weekends. While many have long summer vacations, they use much of that time to organize materials, order supplies, preview films and other resources, see new products, and attend classes to improve their skills. Although teachers are only in the classroom until mid-afternoon, school libraries are usually open for students after school hours, so library media specialist schedules reflect the basic nine-to-five workday.

Many library media centers are understaffed. Library media specialists might have to perform clerical duties, such as shelving books, in addition to their normal responsibilities. They might have to serve the library media centers in more than one building. In some cases, they might face the daunting task of being the only library media specialist available to serve hundreds or even thousands of students and their teachers.

Some might experience stress when dealing with the pressure of keeping up with the latest technological advances. However, new developments in information technology and their applications to the learning process will keep the work of library media specialists both interesting and challenging.

OUTLOOK

The American Library Association predicts that opportunities for library media specialists should be good in the next decade. More openings are expected in library media centers in schools, as well as in media centers in public libraries and in other organizations. As the use of computers continues to spread in classrooms and in library media centers, library media specialists who have developed excellent computer skills might move into such positions as computer coordinator for the entire school or school district.

Library media specialists who have worked in schools will also find opportunities to take their educational background into jobs with educational product companies as software producers or as researchers who help their firms determine the materials that schools need. They may also utilize their background in children's and young-adult literature by working for publishing companies.

In addition, there will be increasing opportunities for library media specialists who wish to take their skills from the school and library setting into the outside world of business, industry, medical establishments, and government organizations. These alternative settings will allow experienced specialists to use media materials to train workers and to spread their messages to the public. Media skills will prove valuable to those wishing to move into advertising and public relations. Some media specialists will find work with health and welfare services to develop materials that teach people how to maintain their health and spend money wisely.

FOR MORE INFORMATION

For career information and a list of accredited educational programs, contact

American Association of School Librarians
c/o American Library Association
50 East Huron Street
Chicago, IL 60611-2795
Tel: 800-545-2433, ext. 4382
E-mail: aasl@ala.org
http://www.ala.org/ala/mgrps/divs/aasl

For a list of accredited schools and information on careers, scholarships and grants, and membership, contact
American Library Association
50 East Huron Street
Chicago, IL 60611-2729
Tel: 800-545-2433
http://www.ala.org

To learn more about information science careers, contact
American Society for Information Science and Technology
1320 Fenwick Lane, Suite 510
Silver Spring, MD 20910-3560
Tel: 301-495-0900
E-mail: asis@asis.org
http://www.asis.org

For information on education and awards programs, contact
Association for Educational Communications and Technology
PO Box 2447
Bloomington, IN 47402-2447
Tel: 877-677-2328
E-mail: aect@aect.org
http://www.aect.org

For information on a career as a children's librarian, contact
Association for Library Service to Children
c/o American Library Association
50 East Huron Street
Chicago, IL 60611-2795
Tel: 800-545-2433, ext. 2163
E-mail: alsc@ala.org
http://www.ala.org/ala/mgrps/divs/alsc

The association is a membership organization for media technology centers.
National Association of Media and Technology Centers
PO Box 9844
Cedar Rapids, IA 52409-9844
Tel: 319-654-0608
http://www.namtc.org

For career information about librarians who provide services to students ages 12–18, visit
Young Adult Library Services Association
c/o American Library Association
50 East Huron Street
Chicago, IL 60611-2795
Tel: 800-545-2433, ext. 4390
E-mail: YALSA@ala.org
http://www.ala.org/ala/mgrps/divs/yalsa/yalsa.cfm

Library Technicians

QUICK FACTS

School Subjects
Computer science
English

Personal Skills
Following instructions
Helping/teaching
Technical/scientific

Work Environment
Primarily indoors
Primarily one location

Minimum Education Level
Associate's degree

Salary Range
$17,560 to $29,570 to
$46,470+

Certification or Licensing
Voluntary

Outlook
About as fast as the average

DOT
100

GOE
12.03.04

NOC
5211

O*NET-SOC
25-4031.00

OVERVIEW

Library technicians, sometimes called *library technical assistants*, work in all areas of library services, supporting professional librarians or working independently to help people access information. They order and catalog books, help library patrons locate materials, and make the library's services and facilities readily available. Technicians verify bibliographic information on orders, and perform basic cataloging of materials received. They answer routine questions about library services and refer questions requiring professional help to librarians. Technicians also help with circulation desk operations and oversee the work of stack workers, library aides, and other clerical workers. They circulate audiovisual equipment and materials and inspect items upon return. Approximately 120,600 library technicians are employed in the United States.

HISTORY

The earliest libraries, referred to in Egyptian manuscripts, date from 3000 B.C. The centuries since have seen great changes in libraries and their place in society. In the Middle Ages, books were so rare that they were often chained to shelves to prevent loss. The inventions of the printing press and movable type increased the literacy rate, and the increasing availability of books and periodicals all contributed to the growth of libraries.

The growth of public education in the 1800s was accompanied by a rapid growth of public libraries across the United States, greatly aided in the latter part of the century by the generosity of philanthropists such as Andrew Carnegie. Aids to locating information were developed, such as the Dewey Decimal System in 1876 and Poole's

Public Library Technology Services, 2009

Library Web Site Features

Online catalog: 90.5 percent of libraries have this feature

Personalized patron accounts: 71.7 percent

Online reference services: 68.9 percent

Library Web Site Contents

Programming information/events calendar: 90.6 percent

Children/young adult page: 79.8 percent

Library staff-created content: 71.9 percent

Libraries That Have

A Web site: 92.4 percent

Wireless Internet access: 88.2 percent

Access to locally produced digitized collections: 43.6 percent

Virtual Reference Services Via

E-mail/Web form: 62.1 percent

Chat reference: 31.4 percent

Instant messaging: 19.5 percent

Source: American Library Association, *The State of America's Libraries*, April 2010

Index to Periodical Literature in 1882, and these aids made libraries much more convenient for users. The American Library Association was founded in 1876, an event that is usually regarded as marking the birth of librarianship as a profession.

The great increase in the amount of recorded information in the 20th and 21st centuries has led to a steady increase in the number of library facilities and services. It is estimated that the amount of information published on almost every general subject doubles every 10 to 20 years. Libraries depend on trained personnel to keep informed about what new information is available, to be selective about what materials are purchased, and to share materials with other libraries as an extension of their own resources.

As the responsibilities of librarians became more complex, the need for technically trained workers to support them became evident. During the 1940s many libraries began training their own support staffs. In-service training programs proved costly, however, and since 1965 the bulk of library technician training has been assumed by community colleges. Now that computers are used for many of the technical and user services, library technicians perform many of the tasks once handled exclusively by librarians.

THE JOB

Work in libraries falls into three general categories: technical services, user services, and administrative services. Library technicians may be involved with the responsibilities of any of these areas.

In technical services, library technicians are involved with acquiring resources and then organizing them so the material can be easily accessed. They process order requests, verify bibliographic information, and prepare order forms for new materials, such as books, magazines, journals, videos, digital video discs (DVDs), and CD-ROMs. They perform routine cataloging of new materials and record information about the new materials in computer files. The *acquisitions technicians, classifiers,* and *catalogers* who perform these functions make information available for the library users. Technicians who work for interlibrary loan departments may arrange for one library to borrow materials from another library or for a library to temporarily display a special collection. They might make basic repairs to damaged books or refer the materials to a preservation department for more comprehensive conservation. A *circulation counter attendant* helps readers check out materials and collects late fines for overdue books. *Media technicians* operate audiovisual equipment for library media programs and maintain the equipment in working order. They often prepare graphic artwork and television programs.

Under the guidance of librarians in user services, technicians work directly with library patrons and help them to access the information needed for their research. They direct library patrons to the computer files in response to inquiries and assist with identifying the library's holdings. They describe the general arrangement of the library for new patrons and answer basic questions about the library's collections. They may also help patrons use microfiche and microfilm equipment. They may help them locate materials in an interlibrary system's computerized listing of holdings. *Reference library technicians* specialize in locating and researching information. *Children's library technicians* and *young-adult library technicians* specialize in getting children and young adults interested in books, reading, and learning by sponsoring summer reading programs, reading hours, puppet shows, literacy contests, and other fun activities.

Technicians who work in administrative services help with the management of the library. They might help prepare budgets, coordinate the efforts of different departments within the library, write policy and procedures, and work to develop the library's collection. If they have more responsibility, they might supervise and coordinate staff members, recruit and supervise volunteers, organize fund-raising efforts, sit on community boards, and develop programs to promote and encourage reading and learning in the community.

The particular responsibilities of a library technician vary according to the type of library. *Academic library technicians* work in university or college libraries, assisting professors and students in their research needs. Their work would revolve around handling reference materials and specialized journals. *School library technicians* work with *school library media specialists*, assisting teachers and students in utilizing the print and nonprint resources of a school library media center.

Library technicians also work in special libraries maintained by government agencies, corporations, law firms, advertising agencies, museums, health care organizations, professional associations, medical centers, religious organizations, and research laboratories. Library technicians in special libraries deal with information tailored to the specific needs and interests of the particular organization. They may also organize bibliographies, prepare abstracts and indexes of current periodicals, or research and analyze information on particular issues.

Library technicians develop and index computerized databases to organize information collected in the library. They also help library patrons use computers to access the information stored in their own databases or in remote databases. They also manage library Web sites. With the increasing use of automated information systems, many libraries hire *automated system technicians* to help plan and operate computer systems and *information technicians* to help design and develop information storage retrieval systems and procedures for collecting, organizing, interpreting, and classifying information.

In the past, library technicians functioned solely as the librarian's support staff, but this situation has evolved over the years. Library technicians continue to refer questions or problems requiring professional experience and judgment to librarians. However, with the increasing use of computer systems in libraries, library technicians now perform many of the technical and user service responsibilities once performed by librarians, thereby freeing librarians to focus more on acquisitions and administrative responsibilities. In some cases a library technician may handle the same responsibilities as a librarian, even in place of a librarian.

REQUIREMENTS

High School

If you are considering a career as a library technician, you should take a college preparatory course load. Classes in English, history, literature, foreign languages, computer science, and mathematics are crucial to giving you a strong background in the skills you will need as a library technician. Strong verbal and writing skills are especially important, so take all the classes you can to help you develop facility in speaking and writing. Any special knowledge of a particular subject matter can also be beneficial. For instance, if you have a strong interest in geography, you may want to consider pursuing a technical assistant position in a map room of a library.

Postsecondary Training

The technical nature of the work performed by library technicians, especially when working in technical services, is prompting more and more libraries to hire only high school graduates who have gone on to complete a two-year program in library technology. Many enroll in a two-year certificate program that, upon graduation, bestows the title, library technical assistant (LTA). Typical programs include courses in the basic purpose and functions of libraries; technical courses in processing materials, cataloging acquisitions, library services, and use of the Internet; and one year of liberal arts studies. Persons entering such programs should understand that the library-related courses they take will not apply toward a professional degree in library science.

For some positions, a bachelor's degree may be required in a specific area, such as art history for work in a museum library, or sociology for a position at a YMCA library. Specialized study in a foreign language may be helpful, since most libraries have materials in many languages, and all of those materials must be cataloged and processed for library patrons to use. Also, not all library users speak English; a library employee who is able to communicate with all users in person, via e-mail, on the telephone, and in writing is especially effective. While in college, you will probably be required to take courses in the liberal arts: sociology, psychology, speech, history, and literature, among others.

Some smaller libraries, especially in rural communities, may hire persons with only a high school education for library technician positions. Some libraries may hire individuals who have prior work experience, and some may provide their own training for inexperienced individuals. On the other hand, some libraries may only hire library technicians who have earned associate's or bachelor's degrees.

Certification or Licensing
The ALA offers the voluntary library support staff certification designation to library support staff that demonstrate their knowledge and skills in library science. Library support staff with at least a high school diploma or its equivalent and the equivalent of at least one year of full-time experience in a library may apply for certification. Visit http://ala-apa.org/lssc for more information.

Other Requirements
Whatever your educational or training background, you should demonstrate aptitude for careful, detailed, analytical work. You should enjoy problem solving and working with people as well as with books and other library materials. Good interpersonal skills are invaluable, since library technicians often have much public contact. As a library technician, you should possess patience and flexibility and should not mind being interrupted frequently to answer questions from library patrons.

You should also exhibit good judgment; you'll need to know when you can effectively assist a user, and when the problem must be referred to a professional librarian. Since there are many tasks that must get done in order to make materials available to users, you must have excellent time-management skills. Technicians who supervise the work of others must be able to manage effectively, explain procedures, set deadlines, and follow through with subordinates. You should also feel comfortable reporting to supervisors and working alongside other technicians in a team atmosphere.

EXPLORING
Personal experience as a library patron is the first opportunity for you to see if a library career would be of interest. You can get a good idea of the general atmosphere of a library by browsing for books, searching in electronic encyclopedias for a school research project, or using a library's Internet connection to access all kinds of information. Using libraries yourself will also give you an idea of the types of services that a library provides for its patrons.

If you are interested in a career as a library technician, talk with librarians and library technicians at your school or community library. A visit to a large or specialized library would also be helpful in providing a view of the different kinds of libraries that exist.

There may also be opportunities to work as a library volunteer at a public library or in the school library media center. Some grammar schools or high schools have library clubs as a part of their extracurricular activities. If your school doesn't have a library club, contact your school librarian and get some friends together to start your own group. Part-time or summer work as a shelving clerk or typist may also be available in some libraries.

EMPLOYERS

There are approximately 120,600 library technicians employed in the United States. Most library technicians work in grammar school, high school, college, university, and public libraries. The rest work for government libraries (primarily at the Library of Congress and the U.S. Department of Defense), in special libraries for privately held institutions, and in corporate libraries. Many types of organizations employ library technicians. For example, library technicians are key personnel at archives, zoos, museums, hospitals, fraternal organizations, historical societies, medical centers, law firms, professional societies, advertising agencies, and virtual libraries. In general, wherever there is a library, library technicians are needed.

STARTING OUT

Since specific training requirements vary from library to library, if you are interested in a career as a library technician, you should be familiar with the requirements of the libraries in which you hope to work. In some small libraries, for instance, a high school diploma may be sufficient, and a technician might not need a college degree. However, since most libraries require their library technicians to be graduates of at least a two-year associate's degree program, you should have earned or be close to earning this degree before applying.

In most cases, graduates of training programs for library technicians may seek employment through the career services offices of their community colleges. Job applicants may also approach libraries directly, usually by contacting the personnel officer of the library or the human resources administrator of the organization. Civil service examination notices, for those interested in government service, are usually posted in community colleges as well as in government buildings and on government Web sites.

Many state library agencies maintain job hotlines listing openings for prospective library technicians. State departments of education also may keep lists of openings available for library technicians. If you are interested in working in a school library media center, you should remember that most openings occur at the end of the school year and are filled for the following year.

ADVANCEMENT

The trend toward requiring more formal training for library technicians suggests that advancement opportunities will be limited for those lacking such training. In smaller libraries and less-populated areas, the shortage of trained personnel may lessen this limitation. Nonetheless, those with adequate or above-average training will perform the more interesting tasks.

Generally, library technicians advance by taking on greater levels of responsibility. A new technician, for instance, may check materials in and out at the library's circulation desk and then move on to inputting, storing, and verifying information. Experienced technicians in supervisory roles might be responsible for budgets and personnel or the operation of an entire department. Library technicians will find that experience, along with continuing education courses, will enhance their chances for advancement.

Library technicians might also advance by pursuing a master's degree in library and information science and becoming a librarian. With experience, additional courses, or an advanced degree, technicians can also advance to higher paying positions outside of the library setting.

EARNINGS

Salaries for library technicians vary depending on such factors as the type of library, geographic location, and specific job responsibilities. According to the U.S. Department of Labor (DOL), the median annual salary for all library technicians in 2009 was $29,570. The lowest paid 10 percent made less than $17,560, while the highest paid 10 percent earned more than $46,470. The DOL also reported that library technicians employed by the federal government had mean annual salaries of $45,480 in 2009.

Benefits vary according to employer, but most full-time library technicians receive the same benefits as other employees, which may include the following: health insurance, dental insurance, paid vacations, paid holidays, compensated sick time, and retirement savings plans. Library technicians in grammar schools and high schools generally work fewer hours during summers and holidays when students are not in class, although these "down" times are often used to finish backlogged projects. Technicians who work in corporate libraries may receive special perks as part of their benefits plan, such as stock in the company or discounts on products the company produces or markets. Many colleges and universities offer their employees discounted or free classes to help them earn a higher degree. Most employers offer training sessions to their technicians to keep them informed of new developments in library services and technology.

WORK ENVIRONMENT

Libraries usually have clean, well-lit, pleasant work atmospheres. Hours are regular in company libraries and in school library media centers, but college, public, and some specialized libraries are open longer hours and may require evening and weekend work, usually on a rotating basis.

Some tasks performed by library technicians, like calculating circulation statistics, can be repetitive. Technicians working in technical services may develop headaches and eyestrain from working long hours in front of a computer screen. Frequent public contact in user services may test a technician's tact and patience. However, a library's atmosphere is generally relaxed and interesting. The size and type of library will often determine the duties of library technicians. A technician working in a small branch library might handle a wide range of responsibilities. Sometimes a technician working in a school, rural, or special library might be the senior staff member, with full responsibility for all technical, user, and administrative services and staff supervision. A technician working in a large university or public library might focus on only one task all of the time.

Libraries are presently responding to decreased government funding by cutting budgets and reducing staff, often leaving an overwhelming workload for the remaining staff members. Because library technicians earn less money than librarians do, libraries often replace librarians with technicians. This situation can lead to resentment in the working relationship among colleagues. In addition, there is also an ongoing struggle to define the different responsibilities of the librarian and technician. Despite the difference in the educational requirements for the two jobs—librarians require a master's degree and technicians an associate's degree—some of the responsibilities do overlap. Library technicians may find it frustrating that, in some cases, they are performing the same tasks as librarians and yet do not command as high a salary.

OUTLOOK

The DOL predicts that employment for library technicians will grow about as fast as the average for all careers through 2018. Job openings will result from technicians leaving the field for other employment or retirement, as well as from libraries looking to stretch their budgets by hiring library technicians to handle computer-oriented tasks previously overseen by librarians. Since a library technician earns less than a librarian, a library may find it more economical to hire the technician. The continued growth of special libraries in medical, business, and law organizations will lead to growing opportunities for technicians who develop specialized skills. A technician who has excellent computer skills and is able to learn quickly will be highly employable, as will a technician who shows the drive to gain advanced degrees and accept more responsibility.

FOR MORE INFORMATION

For information on library careers, accredited schools, certification, scholarships and grants, and membership, contact
American Library Association
50 East Huron Street
Chicago, IL 60611-2729
Tel: 800-545-2433
http://www.ala.org

For information on education and awards programs, contact
Association for Educational Communications and Technology
PO Box 2447
Bloomington, IN 47402-2447
Tel: 877-677-2328
E-mail: aect@aect.org
http://www.aect.org

For information on library support education and careers, contact
Council on Library/Media Technicians
PO Box 42048
Mesa, AZ 85274-2048
http://colt.ucr.edu

For information on continuing education programs and publications, contact
Library & Information Technology Association
c/o American Library Association
50 East Huron Street
Chicago, IL 60611-2795
Tel: 800-545-2433, ext. 4270
E-mail: lita@ala.org
http://www.lita.org/ala/mgrps/divs/lita/index.cfm

For information on the wide variety of careers in special libraries, contact
Special Libraries Association
331 South Patrick Street
Alexandria, VA 22314-3501
Tel: 703-647-4900
E-mail: sla@sla.org
http://www.sla.org

For information on library technician careers in Canada, contact the following organizations:
Alberta Association of Library Technicians
PO Box 700
Edmonton, AB T5J 2L4 Canada
Tel: 866-350-2258
http://www.aalt.org

Ontario Association of Library Technicians
1500 Upper Middle Road West
PO Box 76010
Oakville, ON, L6M 3H5 Canada
E-mail: info@oaltabo.on.ca
http://www.oaltabo.on.ca

For information on library careers in Canada, contact
Canadian Library Association
1150 Morrison Drive, Suite 400
Ottawa, ON K2H 8S9 Canada
Tel: 613-232-9625
E-mail: info@cla.ca
http://www.cla.ca

Medical Librarians

OVERVIEW

Medical librarians, also called *medical information specialists*, help doctors, patients, and other medical personnel find health information and select materials best suited to their needs. These specialized librarians work in hospitals, medical schools, corporations, and university medical centers. There are approximately 159,900 librarians employed in the United States; a small percentage are medical librarians.

HISTORY

Over the years the duties of librarians have evolved along with the development of different kinds of libraries and the development of new technologies. As the medical field became more structured as a result of the popularity of managed health care programs, the need to organize, store, and retrieve archived materials, research, and other materials became increasingly important. Medical libraries were introduced to house these unique collections and with them came specialized staffing needs. Workers who were knowledgeable about medical topics, as well as who possessed strong information management skills, were hired to organize and retrieve information quickly for doctors, other medical professionals, and even for patients themselves. These libraries first were created within or near larger medical institutions as a way to store educational and research materials. As research and information has accrued, medical libraries have sprouted up in universities, corporations such as pharmaceutical companies, and large public libraries.

THE JOB

Much of a medical librarian's job is similar to the work of a traditional librarian; he or she organizes, shelves, and helps people retrieve books, periodicals, and other sources. Medical librarians may also help people check out materials, stamp due dates, collect fines for past-due items, look for misshelved items or reshelve items, and work with electronic media on CD-ROMs, DVDs, databases, or even on the Internet.

Because of the technical and even sensitive nature of the material, some medical libraries are not open to the public. Medical libraries in hospitals or clinics are typically used only by doctors and other medical staff who are retrieving information such as archived patient medical files. Medical school libraries are open solely for medical students and staff retrieving research conducted and/or written at the institution and other locations. Other medical libraries are open to the public, but have limited-access materials that are monitored by reference librarians. These workers must make sure only authorized individuals check out the materials and that items are properly signed out and recorded.

Some medical librarians do not deal with the public at all, instead working on the more technical tasks of ordering, cataloging, and classifying materials. These librarians select and order all books, periodicals, audiovisual materials, and other items for the library, evaluating newly published materials as well as seeking out older ones. In addition to traditional books, and magazines, modern medical libraries also contain electronic records, DVDs, films, videos, slides, maps, and photographs. The selection and purchase of these is also the responsibility of the *head medical librarian*. These higher positions, therefore, have considerable influence over the quality and extent of a library collection.

Similar to other libraries, medical librarians must catalog all new additions by title, author, and subject in computerized catalog files. Labels, card pockets, and barcodes must be placed on the items, and they must then be properly shelved. Books and other materials must be kept in good condition and, when necessary, repaired or replaced. In addition to ordering materials, medical librarians must also purchase, maintain, and evaluate the circulation system. Considerable technical knowledge of computer systems may be necessary in deciding upon the extent and scope of the proper circulation for the library.

Medical acquisitions librarians choose and buy books and other health-related media for the library. They must read product catalogs and reviews of new materials as part of the acquisitions decision process. They do not work with the public, but deal with publishers and wholesalers of new books, booksellers of out-of-print books, and distributors of audiovisual materials. When the ordered materials arrive, medical catalog librarians, with the aid of *medical catalogers*, classify the items by medical field, assign classification numbers, and prepare computer records to help users locate the materials. Since libraries have computerized the acquisitions and cataloging functions, it is now possible for the user to retrieve materials faster, using small computer terminals.

Medical bibliographers usually work in research libraries, compiling lists of books, periodicals, articles, and audiovisual materials on selected topics in the health field. They also recommend the purchase of new materials.

REQUIREMENTS

High School

If you are interested in becoming a medical librarian, be sure to take a full college preparatory course load. Focus on classes such as anatomy, biology, chemistry, and physics. Learning how to use a computer and conduct basic research in a library is essential. Developing these skills will not only aid in your future library work, but will also help you during college and graduate school.

Postsecondary Training

If you are set on becoming a medical librarian, focus on science and health classes but also take broader curriculum such as English, foreign language, and history. These classes will help develop your research and writing skills—keys to becoming a good librarian. Most library schools don't require specific undergraduate courses for acceptance, but a good academic record and reading knowledge of at least one foreign language is usually required. You should also consider taking classes that strengthen your skills in communications, writing, research methods, collection organization, and customer service, as well as maintenance and conservation.

Upon receiving your bachelor's degree, you will need to earn a master's degree to become a librarian. The degree is generally known as a master's of library science (M.L.S.), but in some institutions it may be referred to by a different title, such as a master's of library and information science (M.L.I.S.). You should plan to attend a graduate school of library and information science that is accredited by the American Library Association (ALA). Currently, there are nearly 50 ALA-accredited master's programs. Some libraries do not consider job applicants who attended a nonaccredited school.

Because they work with such specialized materials, medical librarians must have a very strong background in the area in which they wish to work. Librarians working in the cardiology department of a library, for example, should have a different knowledge base than those working in pharmaceuticals. Most medical librarians have a degree in science in addition to their M.L.S. In some cases, a graduate or professional degree in the sciences is especially attractive to prospective employers. For work in research libraries, university libraries, or special collections, a doctorate may be required. A doctorate is commonly required for the top administrative posts of these types of libraries, as well as for faculty positions in graduate schools of library science.

Certification or Licensing
The Medical Library Association (MLA) offers credentialing through membership in the Academy of Health Information Professionals (AHIP). Candidates submit a portfolio of their professional activities, which qualifies them for membership. Membership must be renewed every five years so continuing education is recommended. According to the AHIP, earnings for credentialed medical librarians are anywhere from 5 to 30 percent higher than that of noncredentialed medical librarians.

Other Requirements
Medical librarians who work around people must have good interpersonal and communication skills. Sometimes the medical librarian has to figure out what the patron is looking for, say an obscure study on the effects of radiation therapy on a rare form of cancer, using clues or bits and pieces of information. Therefore, they should also be problem-solvers and good listeners. Because the hunt for a needed item or piece of information might take awhile, patience and perseverance are also useful qualities.

EXPLORING

There are several ways you can explore the field of librarianship and medical librarianship in particular. As a student, you probably use the library all the time. Make the most of your public and school library when working on papers and other projects.

To explore the work of librarians, ask around at local libraries or your school library if they have need for an assistant or part-time worker. If they are unable to pay, offer your time for free. Experience with checking materials in and out at the circulation desk, shelving returned books, or typing title, subject, and author information on cards or in computer records will be useful in the future. In college, you might be able to work as a technical or clerical assistant in one of your school's academic libraries.

Visit the MLA's Web site, http://www.mlanet.org/career/career_explore.html, for career brochures and a wealth of other information about medical library education and careers.

Contact the MLA, the ALA, or other professional library organizations to inquire about membership options. Most groups offer excellent mentoring opportunities as well. Finally, if you have an e-mail account, sign up for one or more of the listservs offered by these groups. A listserv is an e-mail list of professionals throughout the world who consult each other on special topics.

Once in college, a great way to explore the specific nature of medical librarianship is through an internship with the National Library of Medicine (http://www.nlm.nih.gov). This institution offers associate fellowship positions to college and postgraduate students interested in training for leadership roles in health science libraries.

EMPLOYERS

Medical librarians work in hospitals, medical schools, university medical centers, businesses, and large public libraries—anyplace that holds a collection of health information. Medical librarians work in institutions of all sizes, from small branch offices of major university hospitals to large public libraries that serve many counties. A librarian in a smaller library may have duties in all areas of librarianship: ordering, cataloging, shelving, and circulating health information, as well as acting as reference librarian. On the other hand, a librarian at a larger institution may work in one or two specialized sections, such as a prenatal or oncology collection.

Businesses and organizations also employ medical library professionals. Special librarians manage health information for industry (biotechnology, insurance, medical equipment, pharmaceuticals, publishing, etc.), nonprofit organizations, and federal and state government agencies. The materials collected usually pertain to areas of particular interest to the organization, such as pharmaceuticals or specific diseases such as diabetes or breast cancer.

STARTING OUT

Generally, medical librarians must complete all educational requirements before applying for a job. Part-time or volunteer work experience while in graduate school may turn into a full-time position upon graduation.

Upon graduation, new medical librarians should consult the career services office at their school. Employers seeking new graduates often recruit through library schools. Most professional library and information science organizations have job listings that candidates can consult. For example, the Medical Library Association lists job opportunities at its Web site, http://www.mlanet.org/jobs. Also, many job search sites can help medical librarians find an appropriate position. Newspaper classifieds may be of some help in locating a job, although other approaches may be more appropriate to this specialty.

ADVANCEMENT

The beginning medical librarian may gain experience by taking a job as an assistant, performing more basic duties such as checking books in and out, shelving returned books, and checking the stacks for misfiled items. As they gain experience, the medical librarian can advance to perform more administrative functions, such as payroll and hiring and training staff. Another possibility is to move into a purchasing role, securing new items for the medical collection and evaluating where needs are within the existing collection. Within a large medical library, promotions to higher positions are possible, for example, to the supervision of a department. Experienced librarians with the necessary qualifications may advance to positions in library administration. A doctorate is desirable for reaching top administrative levels, as well as for taking a graduate library school faculty position.

EARNINGS

Salaries depend on such factors as the location, size, and type of library, the amount of experience the medical librarian has, and the responsibilities of the position. The Special Libraries Association reports that the average salary for special librarians was $73,880. Salaries for all librarians ranged from less than $33,480 to more than $82,450 in 2009, according to the U.S. Department of Labor (DOL).

According to postings on the Medical Library Association's job site in 2010, salaries ranged from $36,000 to $125,000, depending on the location and size of the library and the requirements of the position being filled.

Most medical librarians receive a full benefits package, which may include paid vacation time, holiday pay, compensated sick leave, various insurance plans, and retirement savings programs. Those who work in a college or university library may receive tuition waivers in order to earn advanced degrees in health or information sciences.

WORK ENVIRONMENT

Medical librarians must do a considerable amount of sitting and reading to keep informed in order to serve library patrons. They must also spend a lot of time staying up-to-date with constantly changing technology. Some medical librarians may find the work demanding and stressful when they deal with users who are working under deadline pressure. Medical librarians working in technical services may suffer eyestrain and headaches from working long hours in front of a computer screen. Overall, medical libraries, like other libraries, are quiet, well-lit, pleasant, and comfortable places to work.

OUTLOOK

Employment in the health care industry is expected to be very strong through 2018, according to the DOL. This growth suggests that there will be good opportunities for medical librarians. More than 2 million health-related articles and 24,000 medical journals and related publications are published annually. Individuals trained to catalog and organize this information are in strong demand and will continue to be in demand in the next decade—especially due to predicted shortages of librarians in the coming years. Medical librarians with strong computer skills and specialized medical knowledge will have the best employment prospects.

FOR MORE INFORMATION

For a list of accredited schools and information on careers, scholarships and grants, and membership, contact
American Library Association
50 East Huron Street
Chicago, IL 60611-2729
Tel: 800-545-2433
http://www.ala.org

To learn more about information science careers, contact
American Society for Information Science and Technology
1320 Fenwick Lane, Suite 510
Silver Spring, MD 20910-3560
Tel: 301-495-0900
E-mail: asis@asis.org
http://www.asis.org

For information on employment in academic settings, contact
Association of Academic Health Sciences Libraries
2150 North 107th Street, Suite 205
Seattle, WA 98133-9009
Tel: 206-367-8704
E-mail: aahsl@sbims.com
http://www.aahsl.org

For information on careers in medical librarianship, contact
Medical Library Association
65 East Wacker Place, Suite 1900
Chicago, IL 60601-7246
Tel: 312-419-9094
E-mail: info@mlahq.org
http://www.mlanet.org

For information on working in a specialized library, contact
Special Libraries Association
331 South Patrick Street
Alexandria, VA 22314-3501
Tel: 703-647-4900
http://www.sla.org

For information on librarianship in Canada, contact
Canadian Library Association
1150 Morrison Drive, Suite 400
Ottawa, ON K2H 8S9 Canada
Tel: 613-232-9625
E-mail: info@cla.ca
http://www.cla.ca

─────────── **INTERVIEW** ───────────

Laura Cousineau is the assistant director for program develop-
ment and resource integration at the Medical University of South

Carolina (MUSC) Library. She is also an associate professor in the division of library science and informatics, an associate professor in the college of nursing, and an associate professor of pediatrics in the college of medicine. Laura discussed her career with the editors of Careers in Focus: Library and Information Science.

Q. What made you want to become a medical librarian?

A. I did not start out wanting to be a medical librarian. I first wanted be a school librarian. A few weeks into library school convinced me that I really wanted to work with adults. So I chose master's of library science course work that trained me to be an academic (college) reference librarian. Yet, 10 years after I began my career at the Duke University Libraries as a reference librarian, I found myself in Charleston, South Carolina, with a job offer from a medical university library. It turned out to be a wonderful career move for me. I discovered that the same skills and interests that I used as a librarian in the humanities and social sciences worked equally well in the sciences. It is fascinating work, allowing me to make a contribution to education, health care, research, and patient care. There is no faster-changing field than the biomedical sciences, giving me an opportunity to constantly learn new things. Even if you do not have a primary interest in health care or the sciences, a career as a medical librarian is challenging, rewarding, and personally satisfying. And you do not need a science background to enter the profession.

Q. What are the most important personal and professional qualities for medical librarians?

A. The most important quality is a passion for public service. Think of the needs of your users: What services and information do they need? How do they want it delivered? What is the best way to maximize the information's utility for them? You should also be able to network with people and work on committees and departments in your organization. Help the library bring value to your institution. Other important traits are being a good listener; being interested in your patrons' teaching, research, and clinical activities; and believing in yourself and the library's ability to bring value to your institution.

Q. Are you certified or credentialed? How important is certification to career success?

A. The Medical Library Association offers a credentialing program: membership in the Academy of Health Information

Professionals. The academy is a professional and career recognition program that differs from certification in that certification focuses on the attainment of minimum standards and measurable competencies and requires members sit for a test, and credentialing recognizes the time and effort that is required for professional development. Admission to and the level of academy membership are based on three areas of achievement: academic preparation, professional experience, and professional accomplishments.

Q. What activities would you suggest to high school students who are interested in this career?

A. Try to acquire a wide knowledge base in your education. Learning about the sciences is very helpful, but librarians by nature have an intellectual curiosity, so expand your knowledge base to cover the humanities and social sciences, as well as the sciences. Try to develop critical thinking skills. Involve yourself in activities where you acquire information, critically assess it, and summarize it succinctly. Lastly, develop public speaking skills. The most successful medical librarians have developed skills necessary for teaching and leadership.

Q. What advice would you give to young people who are interested in the field?

A. Prepare for a constantly changing world. Librarianship has had major changes since I received my master's of library science degree, and no one today can tell you what the world of medical librarianship will look like in seven years. But if you love to learn new things, if you embrace new information technologies, and if you look upon changes as new opportunities, then you will be on the path to becoming an excellent medical librarian.

Q. What is the future employment outlook for medical librarians?

A. Over the next 10 years, more than 50 percent of medical librarians will be retiring, and this creates a positive job market for those wishing to enter the profession. Those who are geographically mobile will have even more opportunities to find positions in the field. More information on a career as a medical librarian can be found at http://www.mlanet.org/career, including an online career DVD, brochures, and tips for entering the profession.

Music Librarians

OVERVIEW

As prominent professionals in the information services field, librarians help others find information and select materials best suited to their needs. They are key personnel wherever books, magazines, audiovisual materials, and a variety of other informational materials are cataloged and kept. Librarians help make access to these reference materials possible. *Music librarians* perform many of the same duties as traditional librarians, but specialize in managing materials related to music. Approximately 159,900 librarians are employed in positions throughout the country. Music librarians make up a small percentage of this number.

HISTORY

The oldest known musical notation appears on a Mesopotamian cuneiform tablet from about 1800 B.C. Such inscriptions were probably organized and arranged in libraries that were available only to members of royalty, very wealthy people, or religious groups that devoted time and effort to transcription. The people who were charged with caring for collections within these libraries could be considered the world's first music librarians.

Libraries continued to be available only to the elite until the Middle Ages, when many private institutions were destroyed by wars. The preservation of many ancient library materials can be attributed to orders of monks who diligently copied ancient Greek and Roman texts, as well as the Bible and other religious texts, and protected materials in their monasteries. The invention of the printing press in the 15th century allowed books and other printed

Other Opportunities for Library Science Graduates

Some graduates of master of library science (M.L.S.) programs choose to pursue careers in nonlibrary settings. According to the U.S. Department of Labor, the following occupations are popular nonlibrary career destinations for M.L.S. graduates:

- Book editor
- Chief information officer
- Database specialist
- Information broker
- Internet consultant
- Internet coordinator
- Internet trainer
- Online content manager
- Salesworker, software and library-related products
- Taxonomist
- Web developer
- Webmaster

material to be made more quickly and disseminated more widely. Books went from palaces and churches to the homes of the common people.

In the United States, the first music library was established by the Brooklyn (New York) Public Library in 1882. The Library of Congress Division of Music was organized in the 1890s, with a phono-record collection established at the institution in 1903. By the early 20th century, music-related resources gained popular appeal in our nation's libraries. In fact, *Library Journal* devoted its August 1915 issue to the music collections of public libraries. By 1928, 53 colleges and universities had libraries with music collections—although only 12 of these collections featured audio recordings. In 1931, the Music Library Association (MLA) was formed to represent the professional interests of music librarians. Today's music librarians not only manage and organize music manuscripts, books, and recordings, but also must have a keen knowledge of the Internet and music computer software programs.

THE JOB

Music librarians perform many of the same tasks as general librarians. These duties, with an emphasis on music, include arranging, cataloging, and maintaining library collections; helping patrons find materials and advising them on how to use resources effectively; creating catalogs, indexes, brochures, exhibits, Web sites, and bibliographies to educate users about the library's resources; supervising the purchase and maintenance of the equipment needed to use these materials; hiring, training, and supervising library staff; setting and implementing budgets; and keeping abreast of developments in the field. They also select and acquire music, videos, records, cassettes, DVDs, MP3s, compact discs, books, manuscripts, and other nonbook materials for the library; this entails evaluating newly published materials as well as seeking out older materials.

Specialized duties for music librarians vary based on their employer and their skill set. For example, a music librarian employed by a college, university, or conservatory may acquire the music needed by student musical groups, while a librarian who is employed by music publishers may help edit musical publications. Music librarians employed by radio and television stations catalog and oversee music-related materials that are used solely by employees of these organizations. They research and recommend music selections for programs, prepare musical selections for on-air shifts, and maintain relationships with record companies and distributors.

Some music librarians may arrange special music-related courses, presentations, or performances at their libraries. They may also compile lists of books, periodicals, articles, Web sites, and audiovisual materials on music, or they may teach others how to do this.

Music librarians at large libraries may specialize in one particular task. *Music catalogers* are librarians who specialize in the cataloging and classification of music-related materials such as scores and sound recordings, software, audiovisual materials, and books. *Music bibliographers* create detailed lists of music-related materials for use by library patrons. These lists may be organized by subject, language, date, composer, musician, or other criteria.

In addition to their regular duties, some music librarians teach music- or library science-related courses at colleges and universities. Others write reviews of books and music for print and online publications.

REQUIREMENTS

High School

If you are interested in becoming a music librarian, be sure to take a full college preparatory course load. Focus on classes in music, English, speech, history, and foreign languages. Learning how to use a computer and conduct basic research in a library is essential. Developing these skills will not only aid in your future library work, but will also help you in college and in any other career areas you decide to pursue.

Postsecondary Training

Most students interested in becoming music librarians pursue undergraduate education in a music-related field. In the late 1990s, the MLA surveyed its members regarding educational achievement. The majority of its members who received a bachelor's degree in the arts or music majored in the following subjects: musicology, music education, music theory/composition, and vocal and instrumental performance.

In addition to music-related courses, be sure to take at least one foreign language, since music and music literature are published in many languages. An MLA survey reports that the most popular foreign languages (in descending order) of its members were German, French, Italian, Spanish, Latin, and Russian. You should also take classes that strengthen your communication skills, research methods, collection organization, and customer service abilities. More than half of the accredited library schools do not require students to take introductory courses in library science while an undergraduate. It would be wise, though, to check with schools for specific requirements.

You will need to earn a master's degree to become a librarian. The degree is generally known as the master of library science (M.L.S.), but in some institutions it may be referred to by a different title, such as the master of library and information science (M.L.I.S.). You should plan to attend a graduate school of library and information science that is accredited by the American Library Association (ALA). Currently, there are nearly 50 ALA-accredited graduate schools. Some libraries will not consider job applicants who attended a nonaccredited school.

A second master's degree in music is usually required for the best music librarianship positions. Some schools offer a dual degree in librarianship and music. Common combinations include an M.L.S. with either a master of arts in musicology, a master of music in music history, or a master of music in music theory. Other schools may allow students to take music courses that can be counted toward a library degree. Typical graduate courses include music librarianship, music bibliography, music cataloging, music libraries and information services, history of music printing, history of music documents, and special problems in music cataloging. Other graduate courses may feature sections that relate to music librarianship. Many graduate programs also offer internships or practicums in which students can gain hands-on experience working in a music library.

The *Directory of Library School Offerings in Music Librarianship*, published by the Music Library Association, provides information on U.S. and Canadian library schools that offer a master's degree in library science with a concentration in music, specialized courses in music librarianship, or other music-related educational opportunities. A free, online version of the publication is available at the MLA Web site (http://www.musiclibraryassoc.org).

A doctorate may be required for work in research libraries, university libraries, or special collections. A doctorate is commonly required for the top administrative posts of these types of libraries, as well as for faculty positions in graduate schools of library science.

Certification or Licensing

There is no specialized certification available for music librarians. If you plan to work outside of music librarianship as a school librarian, you are required to earn teacher's certification in addition to preparation as a librarian. You may also be required to earn a master's degree in education. Various state, county, and local governments have set up other requirements for education and certification. Contact the school board in the area in which you are interested in working for specific requirements. Your public library system should also have information readily available.

Other Requirements

Music librarians should have an excellent memory and a keen eye for detail, as they manage a wide variety of resources. They must love music and be willing to assist others with sometimes obscure or demanding requests.

Music librarians who deal with the public should have strong interpersonal skills, tact, and patience. An imaginative, highly motivated, and resourceful personality is very valuable. An affinity for problem solving is another desirable quality. Librarians are often expected to take part in community affairs, cooperating in the preparation of exhibits, presenting book reviews, and explaining library use to community organizations. As a music librarian, you will also need to be a leader in developing the cultural and musical tastes of library patrons.

Music librarians involved with technical services should be detail oriented, have good planning skills, and be able to think analytically.

They should have a love for information and be willing to become experts at the techniques for obtaining and presenting knowledge and information.

EXPLORING

There are several ways you can explore the field of music librarianship and librarianship in general. If you are a high school student, you probably have already spent time in a library: reading, using computer databases, doing research for class projects, or just browsing. If this experience sparks an interest in library work, you can talk with a school or community librarian whose own experiences in the field can provide a good idea of what goes on behind the scenes. Some schools may have library clubs you can join to learn about library work. If one doesn't exist, you could start your own.

You should also try to take as many music-related classes as possible in high school. These will begin to give you the basic framework you need to become a music librarian. Ask your school librarian to direct you to books and other resources about music. You can also ask him or her to help you learn more about music librarian careers. Perhaps he or she took a music librarianship course in college or has a colleague who specializes in the field.

Once you know you are interested in library work, you might be able to work as an assistant in the school library media center or find part-time work in a local public library.

Contact the MLA or the ALA to inquire about membership options. Many library associations offer excellent mentoring opportunities as well. Also, be sure to check out periodicals and books about the field of library and information science. A good book on the field of music librarianship in particular is *Careers in Music Librarianship II: Traditions and Transitions*, by Paula Elliot and Linda Blair, eds. (Lanham. Md.: Scarecrow Press, 2004).

EMPLOYERS

Music librarians are employed at large research libraries such as the Library of Congress; colleges, universities, and conservatories; public and private libraries; archives; radio and television stations; and musical societies and foundations. They also work for professional bands and orchestras, music publishing companies, and the military.

As the field of library and information services grows, music librarians can find more work outside the traditional library setting. Experienced music librarians may advise libraries or other agencies on information systems, library renovation projects, or other information-based issues.

STARTING OUT

You will need to complete all educational requirements before applying for a job as a music librarian. As a graduate student, you may be able to work part time or land an internship, which may lead to a full-time position upon graduation.

New graduates should consult their university's career services offices for potential job leads. Professional library and information science associations also have job listings that you can consult. For example, the MLA offers job listings at its Web site, http://www.musiclibraryassoc.org. Other useful library-related job-search and career resource sites include LisJobs.com (http://lisjobs.com) and Library Job Postings on the Internet (http://www.libraryjobpostings.org). Newspaper classifieds can also provide job leads.

Individuals interested in working in musical library positions for the federal government can contact the human resources department—or consult the Web site—of the government agency for which they are interested in working; for these government positions, applicants must take a civil service examination. Public libraries, too, often follow a civil service system of appointment.

ADVANCEMENT

The beginning music librarian may gain experience by taking a job as an assistant. He or she can learn a lot from practical experience before attempting to manage a department or entire library. A music librarian may advance to positions with greater levels of responsibility within the same library system, or he or she may gain initial experience in a small library and then advance by transferring to a larger or more specialized library. Within a large library, promotions to higher positions are possible (for example, to the supervision of a department). Experienced music librarians with the necessary qualifications may advance to positions in library administration, such as *music library director*, who is at the head of a typical music library organizational scheme.

EARNINGS

Salaries for music librarians depend on such factors as the location, size, and type of library, the amount of experience the librarian has, and the responsibilities of the position. The Special Libraries Association reports that the average salary for special librarians (including music librarians) was $73,880. Salaries for all librarians ranged from less than $33,480 to more than $82,450 in 2009, according to the U.S. Department of Labor (DOL).

Most music librarians receive a full benefits package. This may include paid vacation time, compensated sick leave, holiday pay, health insurance, and retirement savings programs. Librarians who work in a college or university library may receive tuition waivers to help them earn advanced degrees in music or related fields.

WORK ENVIRONMENT

Music libraries are typically comfortable and pleasant places to work. Music librarians may find work conditions occasionally demanding when they deal with users who are working under deadline pressure. Librarians working as music catalogers may suffer eyestrain and headaches from working long hours at a computer screen.

Most music librarians work typical 35- to 40-hour weeks, although some music libraries are also open on weekends and evenings to accommodate the schedules of their users. In these settings, music librarians will have a nontraditional work schedule, working, for instance, from 11:00 A.M. to 9:00 P.M., or taking one or more weekdays off in exchange for working on Saturday or Sunday.

OUTLOOK

Employment for librarians is expected to grow about as fast as the average for all careers through 2018, according to the DOL. Employment for music librarians will be extremely competitive. The field of music librarianship is small, and there is little turnover in the best positions. Music librarians with advanced education, strong computer skills, and knowledge of more than one foreign language will have the best employment prospects.

FOR MORE INFORMATION

For a list of accredited schools and information on careers, scholarships and grants, and membership, contact
American Library Association
50 East Huron Street
Chicago, IL 60611-2729
Tel: 800-545-2433
http://www.ala.org

For a list of graduate programs in musicology, contact
American Musicological Society
6010 College Station
Brunswick, ME 04011-8451
Tel: 207-798-4243
E-mail: ams@ams-net.org
http://www.ams-net.org

For information on careers in music librarianship, contact
Music Library Association
8551 Research Way, Suite 180
Middleton, WI 53562-3567
Tel: 608-836-5825
E-mail: mla@areditions.com
http://www.musiclibraryassoc.org

This Web site features descriptions of and links to ethnomusicology degree programs.
Society for Ethnomusicology
1165 East 3rd Street
Morrison Hall 005
Indiana University
Bloomington, IN 47405-3700
Tel: 812-855-6672
E-mail: sem@indiana.edu
http://www.ethnomusicology.org

For information on working in a specialized library, contact
Special Libraries Association
331 South Patrick Street
Alexandria, VA 22314-3501
Tel: 703-647-4900
http://www.sla.org

For information on librarianship in Canada, contact
Canadian Library Association
1150 Morrison Drive, Suite 400
Ottawa, ON K2H 8S9 Canada
Tel: 613-232-9625
E-mail: info@cla.ca
http://www.cla.ca

Research Assistants

QUICK FACTS

School Subjects
English
History
Journalism

Personal Skills
Communication/ideas
Following instructions

Work Environment
Primarily indoors
Primarily multiple locations

Minimum Education Level
Associate's degree

Salary Range
$16,560 to $37,500 to
$60,690+

Certification or Licensing
None available

Outlook
About as fast as the average

DOT
109

GOE
N/A

NOC
4122

O*NET-SOC
19-4061.00, 25-1191.00

OVERVIEW

Research assistants work to help writers; scientists; marketing and advertising executives; attorneys; professors; publishers; politicians; museum curators; radio, film, and television producers; and a wide variety of other professionals get their jobs done. They are information specialists who find the facts, data, and statistics that their employers need, leaving the employers free to pursue the larger task at hand.

HISTORY

Assistants have been around for as long as people have worked, and the first time a worker sent an assistant out to gather information, the job of research assistant was born. Although the job of the research assistant has changed little since the early days, the tools used to gather information have changed dramatically. An assistant to a doctor a century ago would have had to travel to libraries and other information centers to gather data on a disease from books and then laboriously take down notes to take back to the doctor. Nowadays, that same research assistant could do an Internet or database search and print out the findings in only a few minutes. As technology becomes more advanced, research assistants will have the convenience of using new methods to complete their research, but they will also bear the burden of having to master the techniques to get the information they need.

Do You Have What It Takes?

So you want to be a research assistant? See if you have what it takes to be a top-notch researcher. Be creative and try to find the following information:

- How many libraries are located in the United States?
- How many translators are employed by the U.S. government?
- How many species of animals become extinct every day? Each year?
- How many bones are in a human foot?
- How many librarians are employed in the United States?
- What are the 13 original U.S. colonies?
- What countries made up the Axis powers during World War II?
- How many current professional baseball players are from Japan? From Panama?
- When was the first public library in the United States opened?
- When and in what country was pizza invented?
- What is the longest river in the world?
- How many number one songs did the Beatles record? Of those, how many did they write?
- What library system has the most books?
- What is the average January temperature in Bemidji, Minnesota?

THE JOB

Although the fields in which they work may differ greatly, all research assistants work to help their employers complete a job more easily and more thoroughly. A research assistant may work for one person, such as a university professor, or for a team of people, such as the writers of brochures, newsletters, and press releases at a large nonprofit organization. If the research assistant works for more than one person, a system must be developed to determine whose work will be done when. Sometimes the team assigning the work determines the order in which jobs should be done; other times, research assistants keep sign-up sheets and perform the research requests in the order they are listed. Often, an urgent job will make it necessary for the research assistant to disregard the sheet and jump to the new task quickly. Sometimes research assistants help with clerical duties, such as transcription, word processing, and reception, or, in the case of scientific research assistants, with cleaning and maintaining laboratories and equipment.

After receiving a research assignment from the person or people they assist, research assistants must first determine how to locate the desired information. Sometimes this will be as simple as making a single phone call and requesting a brochure. At other times, it may involve hours, days, or even weeks of research in libraries, archives, museums, or laboratories, and on the Internet, going from book to book, source to source, or experiment to experiment until all of the necessary information has been compiled and consolidated. Research assistants must then prepare the material for presentation to the person who requested it. If specific brochures or catalogs are requested, the research assistant need only hand them over when they arrive. More often than not, however, the research assistant has to write up notes or even a report outlining the research efforts and presenting the information they were asked to locate. These reports may include graphs, charts, statistics, and drawings or photographs. They include a listing of sources and the exact specifications of any interviews conducted, surveys taken, or experiments performed. Sometimes research assistants are asked to present this information verbally as well.

Because research assistants work in almost every field imaginable, it is impossible to list all the possible research assistant positions in this chapter. Following are some of the most common areas or situations in which research assistants work.

Research assistants work for writers in a wide variety of circumstances. They may work for commercial magazines and newspapers where they might locate possible interview candidates, conduct surveys, scan other periodicals for relevant articles and features, or help a writer gather information for an article. For example, a writer doing an article on the history of hip-hop music might send a research assistant to compile statistics on hip-hop music sales from over the years or create a comprehensive list of artists signed by a specific record label. Some research assistants working for periodicals and other publications do nothing but confirm facts, such as dates, ages, and statistics. These researchers are called *fact checkers*. Research assistants who work in radio, film, or television often help locate and organize historical facts, find experts to be interviewed, or help follow up on ideas for future programs.

Many large companies, agencies, and organizations hire research assistants to help their in-house writing staff produce brochures, newsletters, and press releases. Research assistants may gather facts and statistics, retrieve applicable quotes, and conduct preliminary phone interviews.

Advertising and marketing agencies hire research assistants to help them discover consumer desires and the best ways to advertise and market products. Imagine that a small toy company is considering marketing a new toy. Research assistants for the company might be assigned to help find out how much it would cost to make the toy, whether there is already a similar toy on the market, who might buy the toy, and who might sell the toy. This would help the marketing department decide in what ways the toy should be marketed. In advertising, research assistants may be asked to provide executives with statistics and quotes so that the executives may determine whether a product is appealing to a certain portion of the population.

University professors hire research assistants to help them in their research in all fields. For example, a history professor working on a paper about the Italian military might send a research assistant to the library to uncover everything possible about the Italian military presence in Greece during World War II. A research assistant in microbiology will help a biologist prepare and perform experiments and record data. Often, professors hire graduate students as research assistants, either during the summer or in addition to the student's regular course load. Sometimes a research assistantship is part of a financial aid package; this ensures that the professor has help with research and gives the students an opportunity to earn money while learning more about their chosen field.

Politicians hire research assistants to help find out how a campaign is succeeding or failing, to find statistics on outcomes of past elections, and to determine the issues that are especially important to the constituents, among other things. Research assistants who work for politicians may also follow the opponent's campaign, trying to find ways to win over new supporters.

Some research assistants work for museums where they try to determine ways to add to a collection, develop signs and explanations for public education, and keep an inventory of all collection pieces. Research assistants may also do research to help curators learn more about the pieces in the museum's collection.

Again, these are only a few of the areas in which research assistants may work, and their duties may be as varied as the many fields and organizations that employ them.

REQUIREMENTS
High School
Requirements for becoming a research assistant vary depending upon the field in which you hope to work. In high school, take a

wide variety of college preparatory courses, including English, history, mathematics, and the sciences. Knowledge of at least one foreign language can be extremely helpful in gaining employment as a research assistant, especially in the fields of marketing, publishing, and the arts. Since writing and presenting research are important aspects of the research assistant's work, you should take classes that strengthen these skills, such as public speaking, journalism, and statistics. Knowledge of computers, the Internet, and databases, as well as excellent library skills, are absolutely vital to this profession. If you will be working in the hard sciences or engineering, laboratory skills are essential.

Postsecondary Training

You will need at least an associate's degree to work as a research assistant. Many employers require their research assistants to have bachelor's degrees. When you are in college, begin thinking about a specific field you are interested in and take courses in that field. If you are interested in advertising research but your college does not offer an advertising degree, you should plan to major in English or psychology but take a large concentration of communications, business, and economics courses. Often, English, journalism, and history are good majors for the research assistant career, as the work requires so much reading, researching, and writing. Some employers prefer research assistants to have a degree in library science.

Some fields require degrees beyond a bachelor's degree for research assistants. This is often true in the hard sciences, engineering, medicine, and law. Depending on the field, some employers require a master's degree, or some advanced study in the area. For instance, an insurance company that hires a research assistant may require the employee to take insurance courses in order to become more knowledgeable about the industry. Research assistants in the social sciences or arts will find more high-paying employment opportunities with a master's in library science.

Other Requirements

In order to succeed as a research assistant, you must be curious and enjoy doing research, finding and organizing facts, working with other people, and handling a variety of tasks. You should also be self-motivated, take instruction well, and be resourceful. For example, a research assistant assigned by an attorney to research marriage records at the county clerk's office should not be calling the law firm every few minutes to ask for further direction. A good research assistant must be able to take an assignment, immediately ask any questions necessary to clarify the task, and then begin retrieving the requested information.

EXPLORING

You can begin exploring this career while working on your own school assignments. Use different types of resources, such as newspapers, magazines, library catalogs, computers, the Internet, and official records and documents. If you are interested in becoming a research assistant in the sciences or medicine, be sure to pay close attention to procedures and methods in your laboratory classes.

Consider joining groups in your school devoted to research or fieldwork. Work as a reporter for your school newspaper, or volunteer to write feature articles for your yearbook. Both of these positions will provide you with experience in research and fact finding. You can also create your own research opportunities. If you are a member of the marching band, for instance, you could research the history of the clarinet and write an article for the band newsletter.

Occasionally, small newspapers, nonprofit groups, political campaigns, and other organizations will accept student interns, volunteers, or even summer employees to help out with special projects. If you obtain such a position, you may have the opportunity to help with research, or at least, to see professionals in action, learn valuable work skills, and help support a good cause.

There are many books available describing the techniques of basic research skills. Ask a librarian or bookstore worker to help you locate them, or better yet, begin developing your research skills by tracking down materials yourself. The Internet is also full of helpful information on all subjects. To get tips on designing research surveys and analyzing data, visit http://www.hostedsurvey.com.

EMPLOYERS

All types of companies, organizations, and private individuals employ research assistants. Most college and university professors have a research assistant on staff to help them with articles and books they are writing. Newspapers and magazines use research assistants to find information for articles and verify facts. Museums employ research assistants to find information to add to museum collections, as well as to search museum archives for information requested by outside historians, scientists, writers, and other scholars. Companies in all fields need people to help find information on products, ingredients, production techniques, and even on competitors.

The government is a major employer of research assistants as well. Local, state, and federal government offices often hire research assistants to conduct interviews, gather statistics, compile information, and synthesize data. Research assistants for the government work for the U.S. Census Bureau, the U.S. Bureau of Labor Statistics, and the Library of Congress, among other divisions.

STARTING OUT

How you begin a career as a research assistant depends largely upon the field in which you are interested in working. In college, you may wish to pursue an assistantship with a professor. He or she can act as a mentor while you are earning your degree and offer valuable advice and feedback on your research techniques.

After receiving a bachelor's degree, you might begin by contacting agencies, firms, or companies where you'd like to work. For example, if you are interested in doing research to support writers, you might apply to newspapers, magazines, and large companies that produce their own publications. Also, some college and university career offices have listings of job openings in the research fields; occasionally these jobs are advertised in newspapers and magazines.

There may also be freelance opportunities for the beginning research assistant. Try marketing your services in the school newspaper or bulletin boards of your alma mater. Perhaps you could set up a Web page that lists your qualifications and the services you offer. Ask for referrals from professors with whom you have studied or worked. If you do a thorough, competent job on assignments, you may be able to use positive word-of-mouth to get more work.

ADVANCEMENT

A research assistant who gains a high skill level and demonstrates dedication to the employer and the field may earn the opportunity to lead other assistants on a special project. Some research assistants who work for writers and prove to have excellent writing skills themselves may get hired to write newsletter articles or brochures for publications. Depending on departmental needs, research assistants who work for a university while earning a degree may be offered a full-time position upon completion of their studies. Research assistants who work for clients on a freelance basis may find that they get more assignments and can command higher fees as they gain experience and a good reputation.

Advancement in this field is usually up to the individual. You will need to seek out opportunities. If you are interested in getting better assignments, you will probably need to ask for them. If you would like to supervise a newsletter or brochure project within your company, try making a proposal to your manager. With a proven track record and a solid idea of how a project can be accomplished, increased responsibility is likely to be granted.

EARNINGS

Earnings vary widely, depending on field, level of education, and employer. Generally, large companies pay their research assistants more than smaller businesses and nonprofit organizations do. Research assistants with advanced degrees make more than those with only a bachelor's degree. Research assistants who work for large pharmaceutical companies or engineering laboratories and have advanced science degrees make among the highest wages in the field.

Each college and university has its own salary budget for graduate student research assistants. There are often set minimum salaries for academic year employment and for full 12-month employment. Most student research assistants work part time and receive a percentage of these minimums based on the number of hours they work (usually 50 percent, 25 percent, or 33 percent). Some schools have an hourly rate that averages about $10 to $15. Annual salaries for university research assistants can range from $16,560 to $50,220.

Social science research assistants earned median annual salaries of $37,500 in 2009, according to the U.S. Department of Labor (DOL). Salaries ranged from less than $21,600 to $60,690 or more.

Self-employed research assistants get paid by the hour or by assignment. Depending on the experience of the research assistant, the complexity of the assignment, and the location of the job, pay rates may be anywhere from minimum wage to $25 per hour, although $10 to $12 is the norm.

Benefits such as health insurance, vacation, and sick leave vary by field and employer. Universities generally provide health care coverage, paid vacations, sick time, and a pension plan for full-time employees. Research assistants employed full time by a private company are also eligible for similar benefits; some companies may provide benefits to part-time or contract workers. Freelancers must provide their own benefits.

Research assistants who work in some fields may receive additional bonuses. A person working on a research project about movies, for instance, may receive free passes to a local theater. A woman's magazine may send research assistants cosmetics samples so they can test different lipsticks for staying power. Research assistants charged with finding information about another country's economy may even be sent abroad. All of these perks, of course, vary depending on the needs of the employer and the experience of the researcher.

WORK ENVIRONMENT

Most research assistants work indoors in clean, climate-controlled, pleasant facilities. Many spend most of their time at the business that employs them, checking facts over the phone, finding data on the Internet or in computer databases, searching the company's records, writing up reports, or conducting laboratory research. Others spend a great deal of time in libraries, government offices, courthouses, museums, archives, and even in such unlikely places as shopping malls and supermarkets. In short, research assistants go wherever they can to obtain the information requested.

Most assignments require that research assistants do their work on their own, with little direct supervision. Research assistants need to be very self-motivated in order to get the work done since they often do not have someone readily available to support them. It is important for research assistants who leave their offices for work to remember that they are representatives of their company or employer and to act and dress according to the employer's standards.

Full-time research assistants work 35 to 40 hours a week. They may have to work overtime or on weekends right before deadlines or when involved in special projects. Some research assistants, especially those who work for smaller organizations or for professors or private employers, work only part time. They may work as little as 10 hours a week. These research assistants are usually graduate students or freelancers who have a second job in a related field.

OUTLOOK

The outlook for the research assistant career generally depends upon the outlook for the field in which the researcher works. That is, a field that is growing quickly will usually need many new researchers, whereas a field with little growth will not. A researcher with good background in many fields will be in higher demand, as will a researcher with specialized knowledge and research techniques specific to a field. Social science, according to the DOL, is one field that is growing quickly. It predicts that employment for social science research assistants will grow faster than the average for all careers through 2018.

Although definite statistical data as to the present and future of all researchers is sketchy at best, as technology becomes more advanced and the amount of information available through newer media like the Internet increases, knowledgeable research assistants will be essential to find, sort, compile, present, and analyze this information. As a result of technological advancements, a new career niche has developed for *information brokers*, who compile information from online databases and services. (For more information, see the article "Information Brokers.")

Since many people take research assistant positions as stepping-stones to positions with more responsibility or stability, positions are often available to beginning researchers. Research assistants with good experience, excellent work ethics, and the drive to succeed will rarely find themselves out of work. Jobs will be available, but it may take some creative fact-finding for research assistants to locate positions that best meet their needs and interests.

FOR MORE INFORMATION

To find out about health care research projects and opportunities with the U.S. Department of Health and Human Services, contact
Agency for Healthcare Research and Quality
540 Gaither Road, Suite 2000
Rockville, MD 20850-6649
Tel: 301-427-1104
http://www.ahcpr.gov

For a list of research opportunities and student internships with the National Institutes of Health, contact
National Institutes of Health
Office of Human Resources
9000 Rockville Pike
Bethesda, MD 20892-0001
http://hr.od.nih.gov

For information on research assistant positions with the U.S. Census Bureau, contact
U.S. Census Bureau
4600 Silver Hill Road
Washington, DC 20233
Tel: 800-923-8282
http://www.census.gov

Index